LONDON BOROUGH OF WANDSWORTH

WEST HILL DISTRICT LIBRARY, WANDSWORTH,
LONDON, S.W. 18.

METROPOLITAN SPECIAL COLLECTION
METROPOLITAN JOINT FICTION RESERVE

THIS BOOK SHOULD BE RETURNED ON OR BEFORE THE DATE
STAMPED BELOW.

L.36.

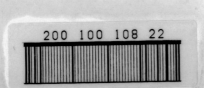

Personality and power

Personality
and power

Studies in political
achievement

edited by
Graham Tayar

British Broadcasting
Corporation

© The British Broadcasting Corporation
and the Contributors 1971

First Published 1971

Published by the British Broadcasting Corporation
35 Marylebone High Street, London WIM 4AA
Printed in England by Eyre & Spottiswoode Ltd, Thanet Press,
Margate. ISBN: 0 563 10599 2

Acknowledgement is due to CASSELL AND CO. LTD
for the extract on page 76 from
The Second World War Volume II by Winston S. Churchill,
and to the HAMLYN GROUP LTD for extracts in Chapter 4
from *Mussolini* by Sir I. Kirkpatrick

The photographs on the preceding pages:

Mussolini	Roosevelt	Nehru	
Khrushchev	Nkrumah	Baldwin	Churchill

Acknowledgment is due to CAMERA PRESS for Khrushchev (photo
Karsh); PAUL POPPER LTD for Nehru and Baldwin; RADIO TIMES
HULTON PICTURE LIBRARY for Mussolini, Roosevelt, Nkrumah and
Churchill.

Contents

This book originated as a series of BBC programmes
first broadcast on Radio 3 (Study) in Autumn 1970,
and repeated in August and September 1971
on Radio 3 (Study) beginning 13 August at 7.00 p.m.
The series was produced by Graham Tayar.

Introduction

Personality and Power was originally an attempt to explore in a series of radio programmes the processes by which politicians achieve supreme power in totalitarian systems. The scope was later extended to include leaders from a variety of twentieth-century political systems, both democratic and authoritarian, to examine their different paths to power and, if possible, to identify the balance of personal and political factors that produced their success. The main emphasis was to be on how they got to the top rather than what they did later. Six of these studies were intended to illustrate outstanding examples of political success stories, the seventh, that of Sir Winston Churchill, to establish what personal factors held back this great statesman, who, despite his enormous talents, took so long to reach the top – indeed, had it not been for World War II, he would probably never have done so.

Each programme was presented by an academic expert, with special knowledge of the subject. We tried to find other contributors who knew these political leaders in their earlier days, before they achieved their individual political summits. I interviewed these witnesses on their direct experience of our subjects' rise to power, in some instances uncovering information of considerable historical importance. Through their evidence, we examined the various elements of ability, family, ambition, ruthlessness, manipulation, assistance from others and sheer luck that took each leader to the top. We were fortunate enough in most cases to find living contributors whose memories and experiences went far back into the early lives of our subjects, among them Adolf Berle who remembered Roosevelt nearly sixty years before as Assistant Secretary of the Navy; Lord Brockway, who first met Nehru in Cambridge in 1912; Rev. Sandy Fraser, who was Nkrumah's schoolmaster;

Viscountess Davidson, whose mother played tennis with Baldwin when he was a shy teenager; Sir Harry Verney, who was a contemporary of Churchill at Harrow in the early 1890s; and Sir Oswald Mosley, who contributed most valuably to four of the programmes. There were only two exceptions, Khrushchev's early career in the frightening obscurity of Stalinist Russia, and Mussolini's rise in Italy before 1922; both took place under conditions too remote for us to find any surviving English-speaking eyewitnesses.

In the final discussion, two consultant psychiatrists and two eminent political scientists ranged all over the earlier programmes and much further afield, discussing a hypothesis on the personality make-up of successful political leaders, and searching for any common factors in their success. They set a fitting and stimulating seal on a series which was fascinating to produce.

I am immensely grateful to all who took part, especially so to the distinguished scholars who presented the programmes, and most of all to Dr Norman Hunt, who opened the series with Baldwin, concluded it with a superb piece of creative chairmanship, and advised generally on many aspects of the programmes.

It is pleasing that these broadcasts are now to have a more permanent life. Apart from a few very minor textual emendations for greater clarity, they remain in their original form. So *Personality and Power* must be read and considered not as a set of carefully prepared essays, but as a record of the spoken – and often unscripted – word. One hopes that what emerges was worth saying then – and reading now.

GRAHAM TAYAR

1 Stanley Baldwin
1867-1947

Prime Minister of the U.K.
1923-4, 1924-9, 1935-7

Dr Norman Hunt Politics is about power and the men who seek it. Some
are successful, like Disraeli who when he first became Prime
Minister said, 'Yes, I've got to the top of the greasy pole'. Others
apparently just as able and ambitious never get off the ground. In
this series of programmes we focus on seven men who did get to
the top of their respective greasy poles, in different countries, in
different political systems, at different times. And we ask why and
how each man managed it. Ability? Ambition? Dedication?
Manipulation of the system? Luck? And in the final programme we
search for any common ingredients in their success.

We start in this programme with Stanley Baldwin – three times
Prime Minister – on the surface, indolent and unambitious. 'A
man of the utmost insignificance', Lord Curzon called him. Yet for
good or ill, he dominated British politics in the 1920s and 30s.

Stanley Baldwin I am speaking to you all tonight as Prime Minister.
Only yesterday, Mr Ramsey MacDonald, whose health is no
longer equal to the strain of the exacting post, resigned and I
received the King's command to form a government.

My first thought tonight is one of profound satisfaction that the
National Government goes on. If the last four years have taught me
anything they have impressed upon my mind the great value to the
nation of a government composed of men of goodwill drawn from
all three parties and pledged to work together in co-operation for
the good, not of any one class, but for the benefit of the nation as a
whole.

Dr Norman Hunt In that 1935 Baldwin broadcast we can certainly get
something of the flavour and skill of this man – indeed of his con-
tentment with power. But he was late, very late in tackling the
greasy pole.

He was born in 1867, the only child of a Worcester ironfounder. Viscountess Davidson, a close and life-long friend of Baldwin's, tells now of her mother's recollection of playing tennis at a friend's house with the young Stanley Baldwin, then aged seventeen.

Viscountess Davidson My mother, who died three years ago aged 102 and a month, remembered that quite well and she must have been a couple of years older than he was. But I remember her telling me that her friends said, 'Well, we've asked young Stanley Baldwin over; he's an only child. He's very quiet and shy, but I think you'll like him.'

Dr Norman Hunt So as a young man Baldwin didn't appear to be an ambitious or forceful personality. Indeed, he was over forty before he became a Member of Parliament in 1908. Then on the sudden death of his father, who was M.P. for Bewdley, the middle-aged Stanley was immediately nominated his successor by the Bewdley Conservatives – and elected unopposed, the Liberals out of courtesy and respect deciding not to contest the seat. So his first success was more a gift and a duty than the result of determined struggle.

But does this mean Stanley Baldwin was not an ambitious man? Well, before 1908, Stanley Baldwin had made two earlier unsuccessful attempts to get into the House of Commons. He was defeated at Kidderminster in 1906 and very soon afterwards failed to secure nomination for Worcester City. So he couldn't have been without ambition even if some of the push at this time came from his wife. Perhaps one of his former colleagues, Lord Swinton, comes nearest to the mark when he says of Baldwin:

Lord Swinton Oh I think everybody who's in politics wants to get to the top. I think Asquith's father once said of Bonar that 'he was meekly ambitious'. Yes, yes, probably he was ambitious in that sense.

Dr Norman Hunt So in Lord Swinton's view Baldwin was meekly ambitious. And Lady Davidson summed him up like this at this time:

Viscountess Davidson I think he was a middle-aged man who'd been very successful in his business. He'd run his business extremely well. He was very honest, very sincere and rather automatically had gone into the political world after his father had died, but I don't think it had entered his head, I don't think there was any ambition to rise to the top; his ambition was to do a good job of work, as a Member of Parliament.

Dr Norman Hunt Whatever the extent of Baldwin's ambitions at this point, the fact is that he didn't make much of a mark on the politics of the time. Certainly he didn't seem to be in a hurry to get to the top. Of course these years before the First World War were dominated by Mr Asquith and the Liberal Government. But Baldwin seldom spoke in the House and certainly attracted little attention. His early career bore all the hall-marks of an undistinguished back-bencher. Lord Swinton emphasises Baldwin's early parliamentary obscurity.

Lord Swinton He was really almost unknown. I think he was in the House for five or six years on the back benches, only making an odd speech or two.

Dr Norman Hunt And then comes turning point number one in Baldwin's career – the crucial first real move up the greasy pole. It was 1916, the middle of the First World War. Baldwin was almost fifty. On the formation of Lloyd George's Coalition Government, the leader of the Conservative party, Bonar Law, chose Baldwin to be his Parliamentary Private Secretary. Now why? It was partly because Bonar Law had been a friend of Baldwin's father. But it was Lady Davidson's husband, J. C. C. Davidson, who proposed to Bonar Law that their close and intimate friend Stanley Baldwin should be his Parliamentary Private Secretary. We asked Lady Davidson what lay behind her husband's action.

Viscountess Davidson Well I think, in his book he said that one of Baldwin's qualifications for position as P.P.S. was that he could give his full time to the job, and above all keep his mouth shut. He thought he had the qualifications and the knowledge and the integrity, and all the other things that are required to make a good P.S. particularly to a rather sensitive – not difficult, no – but a sensitive man such as Bonar Law; and he knew Bonar Law liked Baldwin very much himself. That I think is the real answer.

Dr Norman Hunt If you want to get on, clearly it's a help to find yourself close to those with real power. And it wasn't long before Bonar Law gave his protégé Baldwin another leg-up, making him one of his junior ministers at the Treasury in 1917. Still – that's a very long way from the top of the greasy pole. And Baldwin was now fifty – while Prime Minister Lloyd George, himself still only in his early fifties, seemed set to dominate British Government for another decade at least. And in Baldwin's own Conservative Party were men like Balfour, Austen Chamberlain and Birkenhead – not to mention Bonar Law – all men of ambition and outstanding ability, all seemingly far better placed and equipped than Baldwin to succeed in any struggle for the top job.

But the next crucial point on the way up the greasy pole was the Carlton Club meeting of Conservative Members of Parliament in October 1922, when Lloyd George was still Prime Minister at the head of a Liberal-Conservative Coalition Government. Lord Swinton indicates its significance in Baldwin's progress to Number 10.

Lord Swinton Why he became Prime Minister was the outcome of the Carlton Club meeting. Bonar Law having come to that meeting and spoken against the coalition, and Baldwin having made his famous speech against Lloyd George at the Carlton Club meeting, that meant that Baldwin had then become a key figure in the Conservative Party, in fact, obviously, the next man to Bonar Law.

Dr Norman Hunt The Carlton Club meeting of Conservative M.P.s had been called because many were concerned with the way Lloyd George was leading the Coalition Government. Baldwin, as President of the Board of Trade, had entered the Cabinet for the first time in 1921 when his leader and friend Bonar Law resigned because of ill health and when Austen Chamberlain succeeded Bonar Law as leader of the Conservative Party.

Soon Baldwin realised that he could serve under Lloyd George no longer. He was convinced Lloyd George would wreck the Tory Party as he had already split the Liberals. So Baldwin persuaded Bonar Law to come out of retirement and attend the crucial Carlton Club meeting, when the Conservatives were in effect to decide whether they would serve with Lloyd George any longer. Lady Davidson recaptures some of the drama of the occasion.

Viscountess Davidson Well, I can remember very well going with Mrs Baldwin and sitting in a car and waiting for them to come out of the Carlton Club, and Phillip Sassoon was Lloyd George's Parliamentary Secretary. And we suddenly saw him come out of the door and half run along Pall Mall with an ashen face. And I said to Mrs Baldwin, 'We've won. Look at Phillip's face'. And then we waited for them to come out, and we heard what had happened, that Lloyd George had been defeated and that Bonar was going to carry on.

Dr Norman Hunt That Bonar Law and Baldwin had won was very much due to Baldwin. He had persuaded Bonar Law to come out of retirement to attend this meeting and to make the speech that wrecked Lloyd George. Baldwin's own speech at the Carlton Club also had a major impact – damning Lloyd George as a dynamic force and adding, 'A dynamic force is a very terrible thing; it may crush you but it's not necessarily right'.

So, the Coalition ended. Some leading Conservative ministers like Austen Chamberlain, Birkenhead and Balfour remained faithful to the deposed Lloyd George and so ran themselves out of the Conservative Party leadership stakes. Which all meant that Baldwin, now aged fifty-five, suddenly found himself in the very front rank of the Tory Party. And when Bonar Law formed his government after winning the 1922 election and made Baldwin his Chancellor of the Exchequer, Baldwin and Lord Curzon, who was the Foreign Secretary, were the only possible successors to Bonar Law should ill health again enforce his retirement, which it did in May 1923.

Viscountess Davidson There were really only two names. One was Stanley Baldwin and the other was Lord Curzon and there were many people, like my husband, who felt that it was not the time for a peer to become Prime Minister. Although Curzon was a remarkable man in many ways, in a sense he might not have been altogether suitable and so Baldwin eventually became Prime Minister.

Dr Norman Hunt But it wasn't quite as simple as that. Bonar Law made no recommendation to the King about a successor. George the Fifth agonised a good deal in deciding between Baldwin and Curzon. He took advice, and among the advice proffered was that of Baldwin's close friend Davidson again. Davidson was now Bonar Law's Private Secretary. At the invitation of Lord Stamfordham, the King's Private Secretary, he wrote a memorandum recommending that Baldwin be chosen. It was his own personal view but it might have been decisive with George V if, as is possible, the memorandum was believed by George to represent the views of

Davidson's chief, the retiring Bonar Law. Certainly, the King was much influenced in his decision by the obvious difficulty of having a peer as Prime Minister when the chief opposition party, the Labour Party, was virtually unrepresented in the Lords. But there was a purely Conservative Party consideration as well, as Lord Swinton points out:

Lord Swinton After Bonar resigned, he wouldn't advise about his successor and there was a question of whether it should be Curzon or Baldwin and there was an enormous consensus of opinion in favour of Baldwin, inside the Party. All of us – or a great many of us – who were in the first eleven at that time told Lord Stamfordham that Curzon would not be acceptable to us and that Baldwin would.

Dr Norman Hunt So the King chose Baldwin, who thus became Prime Minister after only two years' Cabinet experience – the only Prime Minister this century to have had so little previous experience of high office.

But it's one thing to get to the top of the greasy pole – it's another to stay there. And he didn't in fact stay very long at this time. Less than six months later, he recommended the King to dissolve Parliament – though he had got a comfortable majority and Parliament had nearly four more years to run. Baldwin argued that an election was necessary because he had now come to believe that if the unemployment problem was to be solved, his Government would have to introduce tariffs to protect the home market from foreign imports. But Bonar Law had promised in the 1922 election that there wouldn't be any tariffs, so Baldwin went to the country to be released by the people from the pledge given by his predecessor.

Though he lost the 1923 election, Baldwin established his reputation for honesty and sincerity with the British people, which was to be a powerful asset in the years ahead.

Lord Swinton Oh, he was absolutely trusted. You might think he did wise things or foolish things, but no-one either on his own side or on the other side ever thought of him as anything except absolutely honest, and sincere.

Dr Norman Hunt This got across to a lot of his opponents too. Lord Citrine, for example, was former General Secretary of the Trades

Union Congress and on the opposite side of the fence at the time of the General Strike in 1926, during Baldwin's second Government.

Lord Citrine I would say broadly he was a straightforward man. In other words he tried to tell the truth as much as he could. I remember Jimmy Thomas saying in the General Council that Baldwin had told him something, and then Thomas added, 'You know he'll never be a politician, he's too damn honest!'

Dr Norman Hunt Quite apart from the honesty question, his decision to have the election in December 1923 eventually produced other advantages for Baldwin and the Conservatives. It brought Austen Chamberlain and Birkenhead back into the Conservative fold. And although Baldwin's government lost the election, the Labour Party, coming into office without power, staggered to defeat nine months later. So that Baldwin in October 1924 led a united Conservative government with 419 seats in the Commons to Labour's 151 and the Liberals' 40. Now surely he was firmly back at the top of the greasy pole.

But he was not without his critics. Sir Oswald Mosley, a leading member of the Labour Party in the late 1920s, had this to say of the Baldwin of this period:

Sir Oswald Mosley Well, he was a man of the party machine. He was exactly what they wanted to present to the country at that time. Shortly before that Bonar Law had won an election on what he called the policy of tranquillity. I remember Lloyd George commenting, 'Tranquillity is not a policy, it is a yawn', and that was followed up by the arrival of Baldwin, who was the yawn personified. He was a man who represented above all England asleep.

Dr Norman Hunt Friends and supporters could make similar criticisms, too. Lord Swinton:

Lord Swinton Well he was by nature, I think, indolent and he had a curious way of what we used to call going out of gear when he just didn't seem to register at all what was going on. When the Trades Disputes Bill which the Conservative Government passed late in 1926 was being drafted, Neville Chamberlain came to stay with me at Swinton. And I said to him 'Neville, look here, I think this is all very negative. I should like to put into this Bill a provision that if there's to be a strike – you can't stop people striking – but if a strike is threatened which would affect a number of other industries, besides the particular one concerned, that then there should be a sixty days waiting period during which an enquiry could take place and the whole of the facts would be known'.

And Neville thought this was a very good idea. He liked it, and he said, 'I'm going to stay with Stanley Baldwin at Astley when I leave you. I will put this to him and press it very strongly upon him'.

I got up to London some time later. I didn't put anything into the Cabinet myself because I knew Neville would have taken this up and then I said to Baldwin when I saw him, 'Well what is your reaction to my proposal?'

And he said 'What proposal?' And I told him what the proposal was, but I said, 'Neville told you all about this; Neville went straight from me to you and said he would press this on you, that he was very keen on it'. 'I've no recollection of it', said Baldwin.

'Well' I said later to Chamberlain, 'you are the limit. You told me you'd pressed this on S.B. and he said he's never heard of it.'

And he said, 'Well I simply cannot make head or tail of this. I started on him when I got there before dinner and argued it with him and put it very strongly to him and then we went at it again after dinner and I went on pressing it and his reaction seemed favourable until then I saw he'd gone out of gear. He started sucking blotting paper.' He had a way of snuffing blotting paper when he wasn't paying any attention. 'So I just don't know what he means.'

Well that's a good example. I'm sure Baldwin wasn't lying to me, I don't think Baldwin ever told a lie consciously. But it just was that he must have gone completely out of gear.

Dr Norman Hunt Even Lady Davidson was prepared to admit that Baldwin didn't like taking decisions.

Viscountess Davidson I think he would go slowly and carefully. I remember there was an article on him once in *The Times*, and *The Times* said that Stanley Baldwin was a typical Englishman, his spiritual home was the last ditch. I remember we laughed a great deal about that and in a kind of way it was true. He was slow at starting, but when he'd made up his mind he'd made up his mind, and of course the answer to that was the General Strike. He took a very strong line over the General Strike. When once he'd made up his mind that the Government must stand, he didn't give way an inch, and he backed up my husband and the other ministers who were helping to deal with the General Strike in a splendid way.

Dr Norman Hunt After he had lost the 1929 election on the slogan 'safety first', his leadership came under increasing criticism from the press lords Beaverbrook and Rothermere, and from within his own party. But at the crucial moments he roused himself, often prompted by his wife, fought back and won. So after Labour's defeat in 1931, the Conservative Party with Baldwin still as leader were in effect the government in Ramsey MacDonald's Coalition of 1931 to 1935. And when Baldwin formally took over the premiership from Ramsey MacDonald in 1935, he then led his party in November to a victory at the polls even more decisive than that of 1924, his government winning 430 seats against the Labour Party's 154.

So here was Baldwin gaining a decisive victory yet again for the Conservative Party, and setting his seal on its domination of British politics in the inter-war years. How could Baldwin still remain at the top of the greasy pole, in spite of rumblings in the wings from Churchill, in spite, too, of the failure of the governments he had led and served in to solve the unemployment problem. There's no simple explanation. There are many answers. One was his ability to control the House of Commons to which even Sir Oswald Mosley was ready to pay a back-handed tribute.

Sir Oswald Mosley Yes I should say he was a House of Commons man, in the mood of that time. He had a considerable majority and he would almost pray aloud in the House of Commons, 'Give peace in our time Oh Lord', and the rest of it. Well who wouldn't agree with that? The only question was how you got the peace and on what terms you got the peace, how you kept things going, what the society was you were going to frame.

Let us remember in that time you had a developing unemployment problem. You had a housing problem which was execrable, vile slums which we promised to remedy ever since the First World War, social problems crying out for remedy, and the menace of a possible world disaster in war which we approached without arms or without sense of any kind. In fact, Baldwin was sitting there and saying 'Give us peace in our time Oh Lord', in international affairs, in home affairs and in everything else, but doing

2

absolutely nothing to secure the peace or to secure that stability on which alone peace can rest.

Dr Norman Hunt As someone else said, Baldwin could always hit the nail on the head; but it never went any further. Lord Citrine emphasises in particular Baldwin's power as an orator.

Lord Citrine One of his strengths undoubtedly was his general appeal; he sounded a reasonable man. He was an excellent broadcaster. Though he despised oratory and called it the harlot of the arts, he used it.

I remember that in one General Election, I can't now remember the year, but access had been given to the leading politicians by the BBC. They invited Ramsey MacDonald to speak and give what in substance would be an election address. Ramsey declined. He was essentially a man who had to see his audience in order to awaken in himself his powers of oratory, and he was a great orator. He made a speech which was recorded by the BBC, which to my mind sounded confused, wasn't sequential, full of passion but the power he put into it often blurred the clearness of his diction.

Baldwin on the other hand didn't do that. I remember very well when he broadcast, I think on the following evening, what he said was, 'Last night you listened to an orator. I am not an orator', and he proceeded to give a first class broadcast with all the powers of the orator in it.

Dr Norman Hunt The development of radio was clearly a crucial factor in Baldwin's success; he was the first British Prime Minister who could speak directly to a mass audience numbered in millions. In all this he was greatly helped by his relationship with working people. Lord Citrine describes what Baldwin's attitude was:

Lord Citrine Friendly one. Wanted them to have good conditions. You see, he had the experience of his own workers in his father's works, Baldwin's Ltd, and he was very familiar with their problems.

Dr Norman Hunt No doubt the relationship was also essentially a patriarchal one as Lady Davidson describes it:

Viscountess Davidson I know that when he was a director of the Great Western Railway there was some trouble in the district and they couldn't get to the bottom of it and so on a Sunday he took himself down there, and interviewed the people in question, had a happy friendly little chat with them over a cup of tea and came back having, I believe, settled the problem.

That was the personal touch which after all he had learnt with his workpeople in his business. I was told that they always called him Master Stan and looked on him not only as a director, as the head of the job, but as a friend.

Dr Norman Hunt His real strength, though, was the extent to which he was able to personify and appreciate the values and emotions of Englishmen. Lord Citrine:

Lord Citrine I would say that the general impression I got was that he was a straight-forward man, he was a typical Englishman who understood the outlook and attitude of mind of the English people, and he never showed it better than in the abdication.

Dr Norman Hunt Even Sir Oswald Mosley concedes that his success was because he was so much in tune with the feelings of the Englishmen of the time.

Sir Oswald Mosley The country desired to sleep and he provided the slumber. They didn't want to face the facts. The weakness of our people is that they'll never face facts in time. The strength of our people is that when they wake up they act most vigorously but at that time they wanted to slumber.

They didn't want to face the fact that something drastic had got to be done about unemployment. They didn't face the fact that the world was dangerous, that we had to rearm. They wouldn't face any of these facts, and they wouldn't in fact have a show-down on any of the clamant problems of the day. They wanted to go on sleeping which is one mood of the English people and Baldwin expressed that mood of slumber more perfectly than any other public figure of the time.

Dr Norman Hunt And yet that's by no means the whole picture. For the vast majority of Englishmen the 1920s and 30s were times when the standard of living was rising rapidly for all classes in the community – all except the unemployed. Which means that for the vast majority of his countrymen, new dimensions were being added to their lives by the radio and cinema, the big department stores, the cheap cosmetics, the development of cheap public transport.

What most people wanted to do after the turmoil of the First World War was to enjoy these horizons, forget the class bitterness of pre-1914, and at the same time feel nostalgic about the rural patriarchal England which was rapidly disappearing. These were the feelings Baldwin personified. That explains why he stayed at the top of the greasy pole. But perhaps it was a considerable measure of sheer good fortune and accident which got him there in the first place.

2 Franklin Delano Roosevelt
1882-1945

President of the U.S.A. 1933-45

Dr Gerard Evans When Franklin Delano Roosevelt died in 1945, he had been President of the United States for twelve years, longer by four years than any other president has ever served. And they had not been quiet years; in the 1930s the President had dominated politics in America, and during the war, together with Churchill and Stalin, those of the whole allied world. By the American Constitution, the President is given wide-ranging powers, particularly over the vital matters of foreign policy and defence. And in the American system of election, the character and abilities of the candidates themselves play a crucially important part.

Franklin Roosevelt was not the first member of his family to possess the qualities which the American people sought in their Presidents. For Roosevelt, like Churchill, bore a great name. His distant cousin, Theodore Roosevelt, had been President at the beginning of the century, and the most famous American of his day. Franklin Roosevelt's political ambitions were certainly stimulated by the example of his cousin's success, and the fame of his predecessor helped his own early career. Indeed, some people seemed to find it difficult to distinguish between them. In 1944, Franklin Roosevelt received a postcard from a man in Lancashire congratulating him on still being able to work as hard as when he first became President in 1901.

Oddly enough, for all the similarities of their careers, the two Roosevelts belonged to different parties, for while Theodore was a Republican, Franklin's branch of the family supported the Democratic Party. And for all their differences of character and temperament, the two Presidents shared one talent, for making politics seem a dramatic affair. This was Franklin Roosevelt at his inauguration in 1933:

President F. D. Roosevelt We are, I know, ready and willing to submit our
lives and our property to such discipline because it makes possible
a leadership which aims at the larger good. This I propose to offer,
judging by the larger purposes assigned upon us, assigned upon us
all as a sacred obligation with a unity of duty hitherto only evoked
in times of armed strife. With this pledge taken, I assume un-
hesitatingly the leadership of this great army of our people,
dedicated to a disciplined attack upon our common problems.

Dr Gerard Evans Franklin Delano Roosevelt was born in 1882, of a
prosperous family long settled in New York State. He received the
upbringing proper to members of his class, vacations in Europe, an
expensive private school and college at Harvard. He was an adequate
but not outstanding student, and his greatest distinction at Harvard
was to become editor of the college newspaper.

A year after leaving college, Roosevelt married his cousin
Eleanor, niece of President Theodore Roosevelt, who gave her
away at the wedding. The Roosevelts settled in New York, where
Franklin worked as a lawyer, but he intended to enter politics; as he
explained simply to a friend, he wanted to be President. In 1910
he was elected a state senator from Duchess County in New York.
As a legislator he quickly established a reputation as a progressive,
opposed to the corruption of the city machines.

Three years later, when Woodrow Wilson was elected President,
Roosevelt was appointed Assistant Secretary of the Navy, a job he
greatly enjoyed: collecting naval prints was his hobby and he loved
the sea. Adolf Berle, later to be a close collaborator, first met him
at this time, when as a young naval officer he was sent to get
Roosevelt's signature.

Adolf Berle I was told to go to the office of the Assistant Secretary of
the Navy, who was Franklin Delano Roosevelt, to get the appro-
priate order signed. I went round and it was signed; the whole
process took about three minutes. He was obviously doing twenty
things at once while this went through – I remember a very warm
radiant personality, the famous charm that they spoke of later was
evident even then, but he was also not wasting any time on me,
indeed there was no reason why he should.

Dr Gerard Evans Roosevelt's charm is well remembered by the historian,
Sir George Catlin, for many years a personal friend. He also noted

that he possessed another quality of great use to a politician.

Sir George Catlin It is a quality, I think, of a very great man – I do not know anybody except Lord Louis Mountbatten and oddly enough the late Pope Pius the Twelfth who also possessed it – and that is that of being entirely present. When you were talking to him and he was talking to you he was talking to you – he wasn't looking up in his diary, he wasn't looking over his shoulder, he was giving his full attention to what you were saying.

Now, that of course is extremely flattering and made him many admirers, but it wasn't merely superficial, it was a peculiar quality of vitality so that he had enough vitality to attend individually to people that he met. And that, I think, is the great secret of immense political success.

Dr Gerard Evans By 1920 Roosevelt's reputation had grown so much that he was chosen as Vice-Presidential candidate for the Democratic Party. The Democrats lost the election, but Roosevelt had clearly begun to make his mark on national politics. While he waited his chance to run again for high office, he resumed the practice of law, took a job with a finance company and kept his political connections in good repair. His son, Franklin Delano Roosevelt, Jnr., remembers that the house had always been visited by politicians, and that, as time went on, their visits became more frequent.

F. D. Roosevelt, Jnr. It was a life of knowing that my father was in public life, of meeting important and interesting people. I remember I have a picture of the visit of the Prince of Wales to the Navy Department in Washington in the middle of World War I. So I suppose it gradually grew, as later on more politicians and leaders in all walks of life began to come to our house and to our table – politicians from New York City, labour leaders from around the state, leaders of agricultural farm groups, leaders of civic groups. It was a cross-section of people who were doing things, who were active in the problems of that time.

Dr Gerard Evans Suddenly in 1921, Roosevelt's ambitions for high office went badly wrong. On holiday in August, he went down with poliomyelitis, his legs paralysed, unlikely ever to walk again. His mother never doubted what must be done; Franklin must retire to his home at Hyde Park in the Hudson Valley, and live there the life of a country squire, as his father had done before him. But Roosevelt, encouraged by his wife and his closest political adviser, Louis Howe, would have none of it. With enormous effort and dedication he exercised his muscles, took up swimming to strengthen his wasted legs, and eventually learned to walk on crutches.

For a man who had always prided himself on his physical prowess, the change was appallingly difficult: he was for the rest of his life able to stand only when the braces on his legs had been locked into position, and whenever he appeared in public there was always a strong man placed nearby to catch him if he fell. Yet the change in Roosevelt's way of life was almost entirely physical – as soon as the worst of his illness was over, his political correspondence began again and with it his ambition for office revived.

Sir Oswald Mosley, a critical observer who first knew him at this time, believed that Roosevelt's political ambitions outran his experience.

Sir Oswald Mosley A man of vast ambition, entirely dedicated to politics. One of his limitations was that he thought about nothing outside politics. He had, it seemed to me, no great interest in literature, philosophy, music or any of the major cultural interests of mankind. He was a professional and dedicated politician with a fixed idea of getting to the top, which indeed he did, but without the equipment in economic knowledge and the other things which were necessary to be effective when he got there.

Dr Gerard Evans Those who, like Mosley, knew Roosevelt, agreed that his illness had a profound effect on him. It's been suggested that it made him a more serious politician.

Sir Oswald Mosley His illness may have saved him from many of the distractions which make such fools of so many politicians in that normally in political life there is always a choice between duty and pleasure. And the rule surely is to have what pleasure you can in life, but always give a clear priority to purpose, to duty, whatever you like to call it. Well that problem which vexes so many politicians was settled for Roosevelt because he had nothing to do in his infirmity but to be concentrating on politics.

Dr Gerard Evans By 1924 Roosevelt had recovered sufficiently to nominate his friend Al Smith at the Democratic Presidential Convention. His son F. D. Roosevelt, Jnr. was there to watch.

F. D. Roosevelt, Jnr. He was only able to walk ten steps from his wheel chair on the arm of my brother James and with a cane to the rostrum. It was a very dramatic moment. I remember it – I was only ten years old at the time – because as he reached the rostrum and grabbed it with both hands, and then lifted one hand in salute to the Convention, a shaft of sunlight came through one of the windows high in Madison Square Garden and it was almost like a natural spotlight on this courageous figure, who was licking his infantile paralysis, his polio, and was beginning to resume an active life in public service for his country.

Dr Gerard Evans His name, his determination to succeed, and the sympathy of others helped Roosevelt to resume an active political career. Sir Oswald Mosley, himself a radical member of the British Labour Party at the time, found much to admire in Roosevelt's attitude.

Sir Oswald Mosley I spent about three weeks alone with him and two other people on a boat; we were having a fishing and talking trip. We had a great mutual sympathy really for two broad reasons – he had a tremendous sense of compassion, a feeling that the suffering to which the mass of the people in unemployment, bad housing and the rest of it were being subjected at that time was unnecessary and should be remedied. And he was therefore a radical in politics, he believed in radical changes. Those two great motives of compassion, and following from that the need for a radical change in society brought us very closely together.

Dr Gerard Evans In 1928 Roosevelt was well enough to run for office again, and to be elected as Governor of New York. His political enemies, then and later, spread rumours that he was physically incapable of bearing the strain of high office; his doctors as regularly denied the rumours.

Roosevelt became Governor at a difficult time. Late in 1929 came the Wall Street crash and the beginning of the economic depression which was to dominate the 1930s almost everywhere in the world. The new Governor didn't just sit back and wait for the depression to cure itself; he was instead an active leader, proposing a whole series of reform measures to aid labour, bring relief to the unemployed and obtain cheaper electricity.

The people of New York also approved of what Roosevelt did,

and re-elected him in 1930 with the largest majority in the history of the state. The triumph caused him to think of his own political future. His son recalls how the decision to seek the Presidency was made.

F. D. Roosevelt, Jnr. Louis Howe was of course the tactician and strategist on whom my father relied very heavily, he had great faith and confidence in Louis Howe's political judgement. Now Louis Howe had originally anticipated that the year 1936 would be the year in which my father would make a serious effort to run for the Presidency. But of course no one in the twenties could foresee the great depression which hit the world in 1929 and which had such a disastrous impact on our economy and a very dramatic impact on the politics of the United States.

Dr Gerard Evans The Republicans had held the Presidency since the election of 1920. Presidents Harding, Coolidge and Hoover had succeeded each other in the White House. If the Democrats were to recover the Presidency in 1932, they needed a strong candidate, and Roosevelt, holding a more important office than any other Democrat, began to see his chance.

As soon as his re-election to the Governorship in 1930 was secure, Roosevelt started to plan his campaign to secure the Presidential nomination. There could be no doubt that he was well-placed. He came from a crucially important state. At the convention which chose the Presidential candidate, each state had a number of votes, and the states with the largest population had the largest number of votes. New York was the largest state of all; to have the votes of the New York delegation at the convention and a good chance of capturing the state at the presidential election to follow was a boost for any aspiring candidate.

Unfortunately for Roosevelt, he was not the only New Yorker seeking the Democratic nomination. Al Smith, too, had been an outstandingly successful Governor, and he had been rewarded with the presidential nomination at the last election, in 1928. Smith had lost that election, perhaps for one reason above all others – because he was a Roman Catholic. If the Democrats refused to risk another attempt with Smith, Roosevelt, a Protestant, stood to gain. Indeed, it wasn't until 1960 that the Democrats risked a Catholic candidate again, this time with John F. Kennedy.

Smith had another disadvantage. The 1920s was the period of prohibition, when the buying and selling of alcohol was illegal, and the bootleggers and the speakeasy flourished. The Democratic Party was split between an urban wing which was 'wet' or against prohibition, and a conservative rural wing which was 'dry'. Each group hated the other. Smith was an undisguised 'wet'. Roosevelt had more political sense. He let it be known that he was a moderate on the issue (although Mrs Roosevelt supported the 'drys') and to those who questioned him he replied that he favoured a referendum, letting each side suppose that he was sympathetic to its cause. This was one of the ways in which Roosevelt practised that sacred maxim of presidential aspirants – keep in with as many sections of the party as you possibly can.

But if Roosevelt had few enemies in national politics, he still had to outmanoeuvre the other candidates in building up support throughout the country. His son reports what happened:

F. D. Roosevelt, Jnr. By the summer of 1931, a very small group of his friends got together and – it's a sharp contrast to the politics of today – they pooled their resources, and this totalled 30,000 dollars and this financed Jim Farley's trips around the United States beginning in the spring of 1931. Jim Farley was seeking to line up delegations in support of my father really a year before the National Democratic Convention.

Dr Gerard Evans James Farley himself was Chairman of the Democratic Party organisation in New York, a big, friendly man with superb political sense. He recalls his trip in greater detail:

James Farley I went out along the Northern states and came back from San Francisco through Nevada and across through Colorado and back to Chicago. In that way I visited, I think, eighteen states in twenty days or twenty-one days. And I saw the leaders in every state. They were not all friendly disposed, particularly those from Indiana, but in most of the states I was sure that he would be nominated. When I came back I issued a statement the day after I came back which I read to him before I issued it, in which I predicted his certain nomination for the Presidency and his election

Dr Gerard Evans But when the Presidential convention met in Chicago in June 1932, Roosevelt only had the promised support of 566 delegates, and still needed another 200 to achieve the required two-thirds majority. As the voting began, Farley and his agents worked frantically to secure additional support.

First ballot: Roosevelt 661½ votes, his nearest rival, Al Smith 201¾, the third, Garner of Texas, 90¼. Roosevelt was still 100 votes short.

Second ballot: Roosevelt up 16½. Third ballot: up 5 more. The political leaders were in anxious conference – Smith would not withdraw from the race, but Garner of Texas might agree to do so. Finally a bargain was struck; Garner was to be the Vice-Presidential candidate.

On the next ballot, the votes of California and Texas went to Roosevelt. The nomination was his, as the Roosevelt campaign tune, 'Happy Days are Here Again', roared out in the convention hall. Not everyone was pleased: even some of those broadly sympathetic to Roosevelt had doubts. Some doubted his intellectual capacity, a point made by Sir Oswald Mosley who preferred to emphasise his personality and political skill.

Sir Oswald Mosley Roosevelt was a man of tremendous personality and of great charm. Here was this man paralysed below the waist, a superb looking man, a kind man, a man whom you couldn't help liking, but at the same time it seemed to me largely without the mental equipment – not the moral but the mental equipment to be President of the United States. A man of emotion, a man of impulse but at the same time with a great practical sense in the management and influence of men by reason of his personality, which took him through the machine of the Democratic Party on to the top, but without clear plan or decisive policies.

Dr Gerard Evans Some commentators thought that Roosevelt had compromised too much with the political hacks, the men who ran the corrupt political machines, in order to win the nomination. Others accused Roosevelt, not only of being a friend of the machine politicians, but of being all things to all men, of deliberately and deviously allowing everyone to suppose that he agreed with them, whether he did or not. Sir George Catlin recalls a story of this kind:

Sir George Catlin The story is told by a certain person, let's call him Smith, who went in and talked to the President and put forward proposals and the President said 'Well now, it's most interesting Mr Smith, and I heartily agree with what you have to say, I'm deeply concerned with this, thank you so much'.

And then Jones came in, put forward almost exactly the opposite and again he got the same reply from the President, 'I'm delighted to hear what you have to say, it's most interesting'.

Eleanor Roosevelt then said, 'Franklin, you really do shock me. Here are these two men with quite opposite proposals and you told them that you agreed with both of them. I do think it's shocking'.

And the President paused for a while and he said 'Well, my dear, I entirely agree with you'.

Dr Gerard Evans It is only fair to say that this habit of Roosevelt's was in some ways a very good thing. Roosevelt was genuinely open-minded, willing to take advice from all sides before making up his mind to act. He fought an energetic campaign. He promised action to end the depression, which was what the people wanted to hear. But he was clever enough not to be too specific; he left his options open, so much so that close observers of his campaign complained that he was perfectly capable of promising to pursue policies that were mutually contradictory. His son agrees that there was little sign of what he proposed to do as President.

F. D. Roosevelt Jnr. At the campaign of 1932, there was no indication of the tremendous number of bills that were to be passed later on after he took Office on 4 March 1933. There was no indication of the whole programme which we now call the New Deal. He called for a 15 % cut in the budget. He called for a reduction of the salaries of all the government workers, he called for economy at every hand, and he proposed none of the legislation during that campaign which later on he put through in the form of the New Deal. He appeared during that campaign to be really a very moderate middle of the road economic and political leader.

Dr Gerard Evans The electorate either didn't notice, or didn't care; the promise of action was enough. At the end of a tour of over 40 states and 30,000 miles, Roosevelt received the votes of 21 million Americans and a comfortable majority over the Republican Herbert Hoover. On 4 March 1933, Franklin D. Roosevelt satisfied his ambition of many years standing, and was installed as President of the United States. Things happened quickly in the first hundred days as Roosevelt had promised. Adolf Berle:

Adolf Berle The congress of a hundred days was the nearest thing that

the United States has ever had to a dictatorship. It was a dictatorship not because he wanted it to be but because the chaos was
complete and he was the only substitute for it. The Congress of
the United States followed his will completely.

I recall that we needed some legislation to do some of the things
we thought we had to do and I wrote it out on a piece of paper
and sent it up to the Speaker at the house and got the legislation back in forty-eight hours.

Dr Gerard Evans Roosevelt's actions were so successful that on the day
of his death twelve years later, he was still President. Like Stanley
Baldwin in Britain, Roosevelt reached the top through his ability
to use the normal political processes; but the part which he played
in changing the society in which he lived was infinitely greater.

What were the qualities which brought Roosevelt to power?
Few would maintain that outstanding intellectual ability or the
possession of a coherent set of policies were the main reasons for his
success. His name, his charm, his determination to succeed, perhaps even his drive with which he compensated for the effects of
his illness – all these were part of the explanation. So too was good
judgement in promising energetic government at a time when the
electors demanded action to lead them out of the depression.

But two qualities mattered above all. First there was his political
skill. He had tried not to alienate any substantial section of potential
supporters; for the farmers, the labour unions, the businessmen, he
had words of encouragement. He had tried not to offend the south,
whose support was vital, or the west, where he needed as many
votes as he could get. He had handled the machine politicians
with great care. All this showed his mastery of political skills; but it
was not his only source of strength.

Roosevelt was capable of set pieces of political oratory, but he
might never have become, nor have been able to remain President
had he not possessed the talent to talk easily, naturally, informally
to the electors. No other politician among his contemporaries
could match him in this. Roosevelt could project his sympathy
and concern to his listeners; and he was perhaps the first great
master of radio in political history. This was the beginning of his
fireside chat in September 1939, at the outbreak of World War II.

President F. D. Roosevelt My countrymen and my friends. Tonight my

single duty is to speak to the whole of America. Until 4.30 o'clock
this morning, I had hoped against hope that some miracle would
prevent a devastating war in Europe and bring to an end the
invasion of Poland by Germany. For four long years, a succession
of actual wars and constant crises have shaken the entire world and
have threatened in each case to bring on the gigantic conflict which
is today unhappily a fact.

Dr Gerard Evans Roosevelt gave his fireside chats only occasionally,
when he wished to report to the nation in an intimate kind of way,
establishing a friendly and personal relationship with his audience.
His oratory was a major weapon in Roosevelt's primary purpose,
the creation of a prolonged love-affair with the American electorate.

Other political leaders – perhaps with greater skill as orators,
perhaps with more of that mystical quality of leadership called
charisma – might rouse vast crowds to frenzy; but Roosevelt
needed more than enthusiasm, he needed votes. In four successive
presidential elections he showed himself one of the best vote-
winners in history. And the qualities of leadership that he needed
to achieve power were also the qualities which enabled him to hold
it tenaciously and use it effectively.

3 Nikita Khrushchev
1894-

First Secretary of the Communist Party of the U.S.S.R. 1956–64
Prime Minister of the U.S.S.R. 1958–64

Dr Tibor Szamuely The most extraordinary press-conference within living memory was held in Paris in May 1960, after the collapse of the summit meeting of the four great powers. Nikita Sergeyevich Khrushchev, First Secretary of the Communist Party of the Soviet Union and Prime Minister of the USSR, faced 2,000 journalists of all nations. Quite unexpectedly he broke into a tirade against the assembled Western press. The journalists began to answer back – and the second most powerful man in the world lost his temper and poured out a flood of abuse.

Nikita Khrushchev Obozhzi, propaganda. Ish' ty kakoi . . . Poslushai . . . Ya tebe dam propagandu! Ya govoriu tem ubliudkam nemetskim: eto ne predstaviteli nemetskogo naroda . . .

Dr Tibor Szamuely What he was saying, in the coarsest possible way, was: 'Shut up, you bastards! Trying to make propaganda? I'll show you propaganda!'

This then was one face of Khrushchev – a rough, brutal man with an uncontrollable temper – a face that was to become even more terrifyingly familiar a few months later, when he interrupted the United Nations General Assembly by banging his shoe on the table.

But there were many other faces to Khrushchev. I myself had the opportunity of meeting him two years before his Paris performance, and I saw a completely different man. That was in April 1958, in Hungary. I was then Vice-Chancellor of Budapest University, and had been invited with a small group of leading scholars and scientists for an informal meeting with the Soviet leader.

Barely eighteen months had passed since the crushing of the Hungarian revolution; most of those present were non-communists, and some barely concealed their anti-communist feelings. Yet all left the meeting greatly impressed not only by the man's powerful character but by his intelligence, his frankness, his quick and sympathetic grasp of our problems.

Here was a very unusual audience for this self-made man with hardly any formal education, yet he immediately struck the right note. He understood our feelings, he explained, but there was no need for academics to be communists or even communist sympathizers – they should be allowed to get on with their jobs. By the end he had these Hungarian academics practically eating out of his hands.

A very different Khrushchev therefore from the bully of the Paris summit and the United Nations. And during the ten years when he was in power, the world grew accustomed to seeing a man of many faces, a highly complex individual, who could be, and was, at one and the same time, tough, sentimental, brutal, intelligent, coarse, sensitive, boisterous, shrewd, idealistic and down-to-earth.

Khrushchev pursued his road to power within a totalitarian system, surrounded by perils of which the democratic politician can have no conception, where sudden death and oblivion awaited the man who had made a wrong choice, or even uttered a wrong word. He was a machine politician of the most cruel and remorseless political machine that the world has ever known – yet throughout the horrors of the Stalinist dictatorship he nevertheless managed to preserve some elements of common humanity.

Denis Healey, Britain's former Minister for Defence, who met Khrushchev on several occasions, had remarked upon this contrast between Khrushchev and other Russian communist leaders.

Denis Healey How different as a personality type his is from most of the communist leaders who have been met in the West. I mean, this extreme ebullience, this outgoing nature and I think a genuine faith which he has in liberating the springs of initiative in the individual, I would say separate him tremendously from most of his predecessors. I think that most of the communist leaders are intellectually and politically constipated.

Dr Tibor Szamuely Nikita Khrushchev was born in 1894 in the village of Kalinovka, in south Russia, in a poor peasant family. He attended the local elementary school for only two or three years; he learned little more than the rudiments of reading and the scripture – which he was rather fond of quoting in later years.

At the age of fifteen he began to work in the mines of the Donets Basin or Donbass. Khrushchev, as far as we know, took no part in any political activity before the Bolshevik revolution of 1917. He only joined the Bolshevik Party in 1918, six months after it had seized power. Khrushchev was thus very much a Johnny-come-lately compared to the 200,000 Old Bolsheviks.

However ambitious, he could hardly expect a rapid career. And indeed, it was only several years later that he put his foot on the first rung of the ladder. Khrushchev served in a humble capacity in the Red Army during the Civil War. He received his first full-time party appointment in 1925, as secretary of a district party committee in the Donbass.

Khrushchev had had hardly any Marxist education, but his native shrewdness, combined with his drive, his toughness, his capacity for hard work and his ability – already then apparent – to grow with the job, soon paid off. He caught the eye of Lazar Kaganovich, the all-powerful and notoriously harsh head of the Ukrainian party. In 1927, Khrushchev was promoted to work in the Central Committee of the Ukrainian party. From that moment on his rise was meteoric. When Kaganovich was transferred to the capital as Secretary of the All-Union Central Committee and of its Moscow branch, Khrushchev followed his patron. In 1931 he became secretary of a district party committee in Moscow. Another four years and this untutored miner, who had only joined the party after the revolution, became first secretary of the Moscow party committee, head of the most important party organisation in the country. Khrushchev had arrived.

How had he done it ? To be sure, he had worked hard, but in the Soviet system, and especially under Stalin, this was not enough. It was not sufficient to be energetic, hard-working and loyal – one had to take on any assignment, however grisly, and carry it out with the utmost enthusiasm, without the slightest hint of hesitation. And that is exactly what Khrushchev did. He served as Stalin's faithful hatchet-man, ruthless and unwavering in destroying oppositionists and particularly in applying the policy of collectivisation, which transformed – and ruined – Russian agriculture, at the cost of ten million lives.

Stalin learned to trust Khrushchev's absolute fidelity. The mid-thirties were the terrible years of the Great Purge, when the Old Bolsheviks were exterminated, when the whole top layer of government and nearly half the party were arrested, tortured and sent to their deaths on trumped-up charges. Khrushchev survived the purge. Edward Crankshaw, Khrushchev's biographer and one of our foremost experts on Soviet affairs, gives one explanation:

Edward Crankshaw He survived, I think – and it is a very mysterious question as to how he managed to survive – but he survived because he combined his unique, I think, driving power, which must have been valued by Stalin, with an extraordinary flexibility, expressing itself in precisely the right amount of sycophancy that was needed, and precisely the right amount of I-beg-to-doubt-sir that was needed. Anyone who could guess this and get it right with Stalin was a genius – he did it.

Dr Tibor Szamuely Not only did Khrushchev survive the purge – he benefited by it to an immense degree. It was the Great Purge which finally brought Khrushchev into the exclusive circle of Stalin's closest associates. Edward Crankshaw again.

Edward Crankshaw The purges from Khrushchev's point of view meant that thousands of people in the party senior to him were miraculously removed, so off he went. By 1938 he was right up at the very top, as a candidate member of the Politburo, as a member of Stalin's circle and helping Stalin purge what was left of the Old Bolsheviks quite actively and this is a part of his career that he didn't like to remember.

You could say that by 1937 or 38, it was quite clear he was going to the top, but he was going to the top because he got this miraculous opening, made by removal of all possible competition. And of course in those days he was loudest of all in his praise of Stalin and in his denunciation of the opposition.

Dr Tibor Szamuely Khrushchev won his spurs, so to speak, during the purge. In January 1938 he received his reward: Stalin appointed him First Secretary of the Ukrainian Central Committee. By this time the party and state administration of the Ukraine had already been largely annihilated. Khrushchev completed the job and by the time the purge ended, in late 1938, the country lay bloodless – but Khrushchev had re-created what was in effect a completely new party and a completely new administration. In March 1939 he was made a full member of Stalin's Politburo, the ruling group of the USSR.

Khrushchev remained boss of the Ukraine for over ten years, supreme master of a country larger than England with a population of 40 million. This was a period of crucial importance in his life. It was during these years as a semi-autonomous satrap in the Ukraine that Khrushchev first began to show signs of a certain independence of mind. Although by now an accomplished practitioner of totalitarian politics, he had somehow clung on to his early naïve faith in socialism and equality, unlike the other communist leaders, completely brutalised by the Stalinist system.

I believe there were three great formative experiences in Khrushchev's life which gradually shaped and transformed his thinking. The first of these were his years as a young worker in the relatively free and stable atmosphere of pre-revolutionary Russia. Krushchev was the only top Soviet leader who had actually been a manual labourer; he retained extremely vivid memories of those days.

The second experience, which had left an even deeper mark on Khrushchev was the Great Purge. It is clear that the guilty memory of those bloodstained years hung ever heavier over him. At some stage he must have decided that, were he ever to have the power to do so he would exorcise the dread ghost.

Finally, and perhaps most important of all, there was the war. Hitler attacked Russia in June 1941. Khrushchev too, was engulfed by the new-found sense of national unity, of patriotic emotions shared by all. Was it then that he first began to believe in the necessity of liberalising the system and of compensating the people for their sufferings? Such is Edward Crankshaw's opinion.

Edward Crankshaw Khrushchev achieved solidarity with the fighting services and with the suffering people whom he had caused so much to suffer in the past. And he saw in the Ukraine above all how the people loathed the régime, how they were all turning against it; how they were at first cooperating with the Germans and he must have thought this is not what we set out to do at all. Something is very, very badly wrong and I think I'm going to start setting it right.

Dr Tibor Szamuely It was soon after the war that Khrushchev made his first contacts with foreigners. However astonishing it may sound, this immensely powerful man, this future world leader, had never met any foreigners before he had passed the age of fifty. The first Westerner he met was Milovan Djilas, then a leading figure in the Yugoslav Communist Party. In his book *Conversations with Stalin*, Djilas has recorded his impressions of Khrushchev received during a visit to Russia in 1945.

Milovan Djilas Unlike other Soviet leaders, he was unrestrained and very talkative. He also had a sense of humour. Unlike Stalin's humour, which was predominantly intellectual and as such cynical, K's humour was typically folksy and thus often almost crude, but it was lively and inexhaustible. In his not very new, unpressed general's uniform, he was the only one among the Soviet leaders who delved into details, into the daily life of the Communist rank and file and the ordinary people. Let it be understood: he didn't do this with the aim of changing the system, but of strengthening and improving things under the existing system. He did look into matters and remedy them, while others issued orders from offices and received reports.

None of the Soviet leaders went to collective farms. Khrushchev accompanied us to a collective farm, where he inspected the garden hotbeds, peeped into the pigsty, and began discussing practical problems. During the ride back to Kiev he kept coming back to the question of the collective farms and openly talked about their shortcomings.

Dr Tibor Szamuely The immediate post-war era in the USSR was a period of murky and dangerous intrigue. Stalin had ruled Russia for over twenty years; but deep behind the scenes, his faithful disciples were already jockeying for position in the inevitable struggle for the succession. Few realized it at the time, but Khrushchev's relatively remote placing in his Ukrainian satrapy gave him certain unique advantages over the others. Away from Stalin's constant watchful control, he had the chance to develop his own distinctive personality and style.

Stalin never believed in granting anybody too much independence, and in 1949 Khrushchev was recalled to Moscow to become, once again, secretary of the Moscow party committee, and of the Central Committee as well, which also came in very useful.

On 5 March 1953 Stalin died. The fight for the leadership was on. Khrushchev was regarded as an uncouth mediocrity who presented no danger to the main contenders. He wisely stood aside from the first round of the power struggle. Malenkov, Stalin's heir-apparent, became Prime Minister, while Khrushchev was content with his post as First Secretary of the Central Committee. He knew that the sole possible basis for power was in the Communist Party, but at the time this was not so obvious to foreign observers. Here is Sir William Hayter, then British Ambassador in Moscow.

Sir William Hayter Quite soon after Stalin's death a division of power took place. It wasn't absolutely clear what this meant. There seemed to be a sort of balance of power between the two, Malenkov and Khrushchev, for a year or two, and those who saw much of both of them at that time – and I saw quite a lot of both of them; they were then going very freely about, giving parties and going to Embassy parties and so on – I think we all thought that Malenkov was the more likely winner, he seemed much more subtle, much more calm, much more purposeful than Khrushchev.

Dr Tibor Szamuely Malenkov immediately instituted a programme of liberalising reforms – yet very soon Khrushchev launched a powerful attack on Malenkov. Khrushchev became the spokesman of the party apparat, the guardian of Stalinist orthodoxy, the embodiment of the hard line. Malenkov was accused of a 'consumerist deviation', of undermining the primacy of heavy industry and of defence. Malenkov, without a real power-base, soon went down in defeat. In February 1955 he was removed from the premiership and replaced by Bulganin, a stooge of Khrushchev's.

Sir William Hayter Khrushchev used his position as Secretary of the Party to put all his men in the right places in the various Party committees who do the selection; so that all the people who came to the Central Committee, which was then really controlling the country, were in fact Khrushchev men and they were able to vote Malenkov out.

Dr Tibor Szamuely In Russia and the outside world alike, Khrushchev's victory over Malenkov was interpreted as the triumph of the hard-liners. His past reputation offered little reason to think otherwise. Yet in his own devious fashion, Khrushchev was preparing a much more thorough dismantling of Stalinism than Malenkov had ever contemplated.

The 20th Congress of the Communist Party of the Soviet Union, the first since Stalin, met in February 1956. Without any preparation, a bombshell exploded. On the evening of 25 February Khrushchev mounted the Congress rostrum at a secret meeting from which even the foreign communist delegates had been excluded. Not even attempting to conceal his emotions, he made a four-hour-long speech in which, for the first time in Soviet history, the truth about Stalin's crimes was made known. Khrushchev spared his listeners none of the gory details: secret assassinations, mass murders, tortures, perfidy, megalomania, the destruction of almost the whole Central Committee, the brutal deportation of whole nations – these were some of the points in his comprehensive indictment. The delegates, most of whom had known nothing of all this, were deeply shaken; many wept openly, some fainted.

The secret speech was the most important act of Khrushchev's career. Although it was meant to be secret, its contents were widely known literally within days. It marked a great turning-point in the development of the USSR. The myth of Stalin was smashed, once and for all – and with it the myth of the infallibility of the party. Nothing could restore the myth, things could never be the same again. But what made Khrushchev, a loyal and devoted communist, take this irrevocable step?

Edward Crankshaw The motivation behind his behaviour at the 20th Party Congress in 1956 must have been inconceivably complex. First of all, very much to clear himself; secondly to implicate others by clearing himself and leaving them in the mud, so to speak; then very importantly, to clear Russia of the incubus of Stalinism which he quite clearly must have seen for a long time was driving Russia, the economy and the society, into the ground, and something had got to be done. I think the others thought that he would cut his own throat by doing it. Nobody else would have been remotely brave enough to take that risk.

Dr Tibor Szamuely For a time it seemed as if Khrushchev had indeed cut his own throat. The reverberations of the speech were shattering, to say the least. It led directly to the explosion in Poland and the revolution in Hungary. Khrushchev had no qualms about using extreme measures to protect the interests of the USSR, and he sent in the Red Army to crush the Hungarian revolution. But his colleagues, not unnaturally, held him responsible for all the trouble. It looked almost certain that Khrushchev was on the way out.

But in the end his gigantic gamble paid off. When in June 1957 all his enemies on the Politburo – Malenkov, Molotov, and his old-time patron Kaganovich – united to remove him from the party leadership, he was able to appeal to the Central Committee (safely packed with his supporters), to tar his opponents with the brush of Stalin's crimes, and to accuse them of wishing to re-introduce Stalinism. Khrushchev emerged victorious from the encounter; his opponents were all expelled from the Central Committee, but – a new touch in Soviet politics – none of them was executed or even arrested. They were just consigned to oblivion. Soon after this Khrushchev added the post of Prime Minister to his First Secretaryship of the party. He had reached the top.

Unlike other Soviet leaders, Khrushchev travelled widely in the West, but he genuinely believed that the communist system was superior to Western democracy. All that needed to be done, he thought, was to get rid of Stalin's worst abuses. He was wrong, as it turned out, but by liquidating the most unspeakable excesses of Stalinism he at least made life more tolerable for the Soviet citizen.

Above all, he ended the terror; perfectly innocent people were no longer being arrested every day, and millions of men and women condemned to a living death in the slave-labour camps were released. Sir William Hayter explains the reasons behind this most important of Khrushchev's reforms.

Sir William Hayter He wanted to liberalise conditions inside the Soviet Union, because he thought that under the Stalin terror everything was freezing up. People were so frightened to take decisions about anything for fear they'd get into trouble that nothing was being decided, that no scientist dared make an experiment, that no technician dared try out a new technique, and he thought the only hope of advance, economic advance, which to him was the most important thing that he could do for his country, was to liberalise and set people free to think and talk and take decisions.

Dr Tibor Szamuely Khrushchev never became a dictator – he could not have done this nor, probably, did he want to do it. But his period of supreme power lasted for over seven years. He promised the long-suffering Soviet people a fair deal and a square meal; for the more distant future he held out a vision of abundance and of peaceful victory over capitalism. Above all, he promised that Stalinism would never return.

At first he seemed to be successful. He was helped by a series of good harvests; his measures for liberalising the economy also began well. The unity of the communist world, shaken by the events of 1956, was restored. Then, gradually, things began to turn sour. Agriculture fell back into its usual state of crisis; Communist Russia fell out with Communist China; the arms race with the United States was intensified. Liberalisation, too, got out of hand; writers like Alexander Solzhenitsyn began to produce books questioning the basic assumptions of the Soviet system.

Edward Crankshaw was a close observer of Khrushchev's last years in power.

Edward Crankshaw I was writing about him every week at this time and I was always expecting something to crop up that would be the end of him. And he survived; and it wasn't until the very, very end in 1964 that he, in effect, started commanding, and that they were not going to put up with at all. He started making decisions without asking the rest of the members of the Praesidium, particularly with relation to the new approach to West Germany. And that plus the muddle he'd got the economy into by his impulsiveness and his too grandiose schemes enabled everybody to agree to pull him down.

Dr Tibor Szamuely On 15 October 1964, when the British people were awaiting the first results of the general election, a brief news-flash announced that Nikita Sergeyevich Khrushchev had been removed from all his posts. The news came as a shock to every-body – yet it might have been expected. Khrushchev fell, not so much by reason of his own errors, as because of the nature of the Soviet system. With Khrushchev's ever bolder ventures into the field of reform, the party apparatus began to fear for its own power position and even for the stability of the régime. The party, which had made Khrushchev, which had been restored by him to power, finally destroyed him. Today he is an old man living in retirement. His name is never mentioned in the USSR – he has become an unperson.

But what was this extraordinary Soviet leader really like ? What were the qualities which brought him to power, and which have left such an indelible mark upon the Soviet Union and the whole communist world ?

Here is a man who for long years faithfully served Stalin and was implicated in many of his most terrible crimes. He rose to power in a cruel and ruthless world. It is legitimate to ask therefore, to what degree was Khrushchev himself a ruthless man.

Sir William Hayter I don't think Khrushchev himself is a particularly ruthless man, but I think he was a determined man who had no scruples about using any means that became available to him to remove people who were in his way of achieving supreme power. Once he'd got them out of the way he didn't feel it necessary to put them to death, chop their heads off.

Dr Tibor Szamuely Khrushchev himself never tried to conceal the streak of savagery within him. He all but boasted about it at the Paris press-conference in 1960.

Nikita Khrushchev Kak u nas govoriat . . . er . . . na rudnike gde ya vospityvalsia: raz poimal kota, ponimaete, kogda on v golubiatniu zalez – skhvati yego za khvost i golovoi, ponimaete, yego ob zemliu. Vot togda on, tak skazat', i ponimaet etu nauku.

Dr Tibor Szamuely 'I remember', he said, 'as a boy in the mines I was taught how to treat a cat which had got into a pigeon-cote; grab it by the tail and bash its head against the ground – that'll teach it a lesson.'

Many observers stressed Khrushchev's shrewdness and cunning.

Edward Crankshaw He always had this profound peasant cunning which he revelled in and you could quite clearly see him enjoying being cunning. I remember once at a party at the Kremlin there was a group of Western ambassadors standing round and he said, 'Well gentlemen, here you all are and you were all educated properly, at the Sorbonne, at Harvard, at Oxford; and yet I can make rings round all of you. Why, tell me why ?'

And they giggled and looked embarrassed; but I could have told them why. Because he had this profound instinctive political cunning which must have arisen very early in his life.

Dr Tibor Szamuely Sir William Hayter sums up Khrushchev in this way.

Sir William Hayter He was a great play actor, and the part he played was the blunt, rough, honest man who does the job he's given and who says whatever comes into his head. In fact I think he's a pretty shrewd calculator with a very powerful retentive mind, and a very clear head. He obviously miscalculated at the end. He got, as so many of them do, a misleading idea of the extent of his power. But up to that point he calculated all his moves pretty shrewdly, I think really.

Dr Tibor Szamuely Khrushchev's period of rule marked the transition from the bloody Stalinist revolution to the ordered bureaucratic totalitarianism of present-day Russia. And at the centre of these events was the figure of the man from the past trying to lead his nation to the future, of the Stalinist who tried to do away with Stalinism, of the apparatus man who tried to demolish the apparatus – and who was destroyed by it.

4 Benito Mussolini
1883-1945

Prime Minister of Italy 1922–43

Benito Mussolini Che si esprime, che si esprime, che si esprime in
questa semplice irrevocabile definitiva proposizione. Etiopia e
italiana!

Professor Sammy Finer 'Ethiopia is Italian', so spoke Mussolini in 1936
at the very zenith of his power. He had imposed on 36 million
Italians a simple creed. It was a creed more fit for subjects than for
citizens. It was only three words long. *Credere, obbedire, battere:*
believe, obey, fight. And they did.

How did Mussolini manage to reach this supreme power ? Was
it by luck ? Or was it by skill and personality ? Or was it by sheer
good fortune ? Sir Oswald Mosley, who knew and admired Mussolini before the last war, had this to say.

Sir Oswald Mosley The fortune was the collapse of society. In Italy you
had the complete collapse of society. Following the war there was
universal chaos and disorder. And in other countries you could see
in ratio to the rise of unemployment and the rest of it, the rise of
these movements. In Italy there was the complete collapse and
chaos of society. In Russia at the end of the war, obviously Lenin
and the communists would never have succeeded without defeat,
disaster and the complete collapse of society. So these movements
whether Communist, Fascist or modern movements or whatever
you like, never come into power unless there is a plain need for
them.

Professor Sammy Finer In fact it was not as simple as that. If conditions
in Italy were bad – and they were – then it was Mussolini himself
who made them intolerable. And he did this deliberately, in order
to seize power.

Certainly, the social situation in Italy had always been bad, but
it was decidedly better in 1922 when Mussolini reached power than

when he was born, thirty-nine years before. Mussolini's father was a blacksmith, his mother an elementary schoolteacher. The family of five persons were desperately poor. Meat only came into their house once a week. But Italy too was poor – poor politically, economically and socially.

Three things stand out in the Italy of Mussolini's childhood and youth. First; though the Italian people are ancient, the Italian state was new. It was only thirteen years old when Mussolini was born. And though Italy was governed by a parliament, there were too many parties, the cabinets were unstable, the political class was corrupt and the electorate – half of it illiterate – was pressured or manipulated by the authorities. Secondly the gap between rich and poor in Italy was enormous. The poor revolted again and again in violent insurrections. Thirdly, when a socialist party was founded at last in 1902, it soon split into reformists who were prepared to work with the system, and the maximalists, or revolutionaries, who wanted to smash it.

Now Mussolini's father was a dedicated socialist; and the boy grew up in the same mould. But his temperament was fiery and mutinous and so Mussolini became, not just a socialist, but an extremist socialist. And the first thirty years of his life are those of a total nobody who was determined to become a somebody. Ideas and ideology were nothing. He picked them up, he put them down. Personality was all. At this time he was a dirty, unshaven, dishevelled, womanising vagabond, a magnificent verbaliser, but a monstrous egotist, in overt and violent rebellion against the society of his time. From his very earliest schooldays he possessed these characteristics. He was expelled from his first school, at the age of eleven. Here is what the school record has to say about him:

Record of the Salesian School, Faenza His character is passionate and unruly. He places himself in opposition to every rule and discipline of the school. One personal motive guides him, and this is the principal streak in his character; he wishes to requite every injury inflicted by an older school-mate. He cannot support an injury; he wants revenge. He rebels against every punishment and correction.

Professor Sammy Finer This characteristic of vendetta – the feud – remained with Mussolini all his life. At that time it was his schoolmates and teachers. Later on it would be against the Socialist

Party. However, Mussolini's next school proved to be somewhat less uncongenial and he was a good pupil, and so in 1902, at the age of nineteen, he left it with a teaching diploma.

But teaching soon bored him. He wanted freedom. He demanded action. And so he emigrated to Switzerland. And there, for two years, he earned his living by odd jobs – a labourer, a hodman, a bit of translation here, socialist articles there. He mingled with anarchist and syndicalist and Marxist circles. He agitated. He took part in strikes. He was twice expelled and twice made his way back. And he read voraciously – Nietsche, Pareto, Sorel – retaining, however, only what served his own feverish activism.

A socialist woman comrade at the time, later Secretary to the Third International, by name Angelica Balabanoff, has written of the first time that she noticed him.

Angelica Balabanoff He was a young man I had never seen before and his agitated manner and unkempt clothes set him apart from the other workers in the hall. The émigré audiences were always poorly dressed, but this man was also extremely dirty. I had never seen a more wretched human being.

I soon saw that he knew little of history, of economics or of socialist theory and that his mind was completely undisciplined. His hatred of oppression was not that impersonal hatred of a system shared by all revolutionaries. It sprang from his own sense of indignity and frustration, his passion to assert his own ego and from a determination for personal revenge.

Professor Sammy Finer In 1904 Mussolini decided to return to Italy and he did his two years military service, and then he taught in various schools, first in one place, then in another. He was now twenty-six and still he had achieved next to nothing. At this moment the Italian socialist branch in the then Austrian province of Trent invited him to act as branch secretary and editor of their newspaper. And so, once again the round of agitation. He was gaoled twice, until at last the Austrians deported him back to Italy.

And now occurred his breakthrough. In 1911 the Italian government decided to seize Libya as a colony. The moderate wing of the socialists acquiesced, but not so Mussolini. He reacted against the imperialist war as many Americans do against Vietnam, and deploying much the same arguments. He urged a general strike, barricades, the tearing up of the railway lines, violent resistence to the war by every possible means. The government sent him to prison. He emerged from it as a hero and as such he appeared at the Socialist Congress in 1912. He was now twenty-nine.

At that time the Socialist Party was deeply divided between the reformists and the revolutionaries. Mussolini of course was an extreme revolutionary. On his motion the leaders of the moderates were not only defeated; they were actually expelled from the Party. Furthermore, the editor of the crucial party newspaper, *Avanti*, was made to resign also. Mussolini was elected to the executive committee of the party, and within a few months he was also invited to become the editor of *Avanti*. Mussolini had arrived. He was a somebody. But true to character this was not enough. He now wanted to be everybody. He confided his ambition to the most recent of his many women. This time it was a young anarchist called Leda Rafanelli. He told her:

Benito Mussolini I require to be somebody, do you understand me? I want to be not only the man I am. I want to rise to the top. In my youth I wanted to be a great musician or a great writer, but I understood that I should have remained mediocre. The environment in which I was born enslaved me. I shall never be content. I tell you, I must rise, I must make a bound forwards, to the top.

Professor Sammy Finer During the next two years Italy was convulsed by strikes, culminating in the famous 'Red Week' in 1914. Mussolini, in person or through his editorials in *Avanti*, was, as usual, leading the band:

Benito Mussolini This proletariat is in need of a bath of blood. This proletariat is in need of a day of history.

Professor Sammy Finer And then, in August, Europe was plunged into war. What was Italy to do, to intervene on the side of Britain and France, or to intervene on the side of Germany and Austria? The Italian socialists, as internationalists in an imperialistic war situation, were theoretically committed to neutrality. But elsewhere British, French, German, Austrian socialists had rallied to their governments. Why not the Italian socialists? Mussolini wavered and then against the views of his comrades he advocated intervention on the side of the Allies.

This was a fateful step. It marked Mussolini's break with the

Socialist Party. They accused him of having been bribed with
French money and certainly he did receive French money to found
an interventionist newspaper, the *Popolo d'Italia*, which he sub-
titled 'A Socialist Daily'.

Personally, I do not think the evidence does show that his con-
version was insincere. My own view on the evidence is he acted
from conviction. But the socialists would have none of this or him.
They evicted him from the editorship of *Avanti*. And then they
expelled him from the party. Mussolini was bitterly mortified.

Benito Mussolini Today you hate me because in your hearts you love me
still. But do not think you have seen the last of me. Do not think
that by taking away my membership card you will be taking away
my faith in the cause, or that you will prevent my still working for
socialism and revolution.

Professor Sammy Finer Working for revolution – yes! Working for
socialism – definitely no! Henceforth the spirit of vendetta worked
inside Mussolini, against the Socialist Party. But as long as the war
lasted Mussolini first edited his newspaper, the *Popolo;* then he
served two years at the front until wounded, when he resumed the
editorship. Until when peace came, in 1918, he found himself an
editor, certainly; but politically he found himself isolated, indeed
almost an outcast!

For the peace brought chaos and disillusionment to the Italians
and they turned against those who had advocated their entry into
the war. They insulted the returning officers and men. And these
for their part found neither jobs nor bread. Social revolt flared up
on a gigantic scale. Strikes broke out everywhere. The hour of the
Socialist Party had struck; but Mussolini was outside it. He was
on his own.

Meanwhile, strong-arm squads were forming to oppose the
strikers, and the socialists. These squads consisted of ex-officers,
young blades too young to fight in the war, middle-class youths and
rich farmers, all of whom wanted to hit back at the strikers and
the leftists. Mussolini helped to form them. In the Italian army the
term *fascio di combattimento* signifies a shock troop. These private
bands were also called *fasci*. On 23 March, 1919 Mussolini, still
banned outside the official Socialist Party, decided to launch his
own rival movement. Only 145 persons attended this founding

session. It was called the fascist movement, from the word *fascio* or *fasci* of these strong arm toughs. But it is worth noting that a *fascio* in Italian also signifies the bundle of rods carried by the lictors of ancient Rome. It was their symbol of authority. And later on, the fascists were to take this symbol over as their own.

At this point Mussolini had no coherent doctrine at all except nationalism, but he did have a grand strategy. Mussolini needed the support of the masses. He had not got it; for the moment the socialists had it. Very well. Mussolini must detach the proletariat from the socialists; he must therefore smash the Socialist Party.

Benito Mussolini We declare war on socialism, not because it is socialist but because it has acted against the nation. The official Italian Socialist Party has been definitely reactionary, completely conservative.

Professor Sammy Finer Another point of the speech is of key importance because it contains in itself the clue to his entire future strategy.

Benito Mussolini We must be an active minority, we wish to separate the official Socialist Party from the proletariat.

Professor Sammy Finer From 23 March, 1919, the founding of the fascist movement, to 29 October, 1922, when Mussolini became Prime Minister, is the critical time in Mussolini's life. This is the period of his climb to power. And Italy, and Mussolini's activities in it present a very confusing picture. But in the background there were three salient features and if we stick to these we can chart our way.

First, the country was engulfed in violent strikes which culminated, in the middle of 1920, in a week-long workers' occupation of the factories. This proved quite fruitless for the workers and after it, the strike wave began to wane; but meanwhile the bourgeoisie had been terrified. The second background feature is the backlash from this disorder. More and more frightened or pugnacious farmers, middle-class youths, ex-servicemen and the like began to flock now into the fascist squads; while industrialists and rich landowners began to finance the movement. This backlash confronted the socialists and the strikers, and as it was much more adept at violence, began to beat them. And thirdly and finally during this period, Parliament proved more and more ineffective.

Against this background what was Mussolini to do? He had two

alternative strategies: he could play the game of elections and get
to Parliament in a legal way, or he could frighten parliament by
violence into offering him supreme power. But though there were
two strategies, there was but one tactic: the tactic of violence. That
meant in practice launching the squads into assaults on socialist
and trade union headquarters throughout the country, and then
later intimidating the mayors of the cities into submission to
fascist orders. The fascist raids became wider and more effective
week by week over the next twenty months.

During this entire time Mussolini's skill lay in keeping his two
alternative strategies open. In November 1919, some six months
after he had founded the movement, the government called
elections. The Fascist Party campaigned, but the result was quite
disastrous. Mussolini himself received a mere 4,000 votes against
his opponents' 154,000. His party won no seats at all and only two
per cent of the total votes cast. But on the other hand Mussolini's
hated opponents, the Socialist Party, won 175 seats and were the
largest party in the Parliament. Mussolini was in despair; he even
talked of leaving Italy.

And so he turned to the alternative strategy, the strategy of
intimidation. In the first five months alone of the year 1921 the
fascists had killed 243 opponents, they had wounded another 1100,
they had destroyed 120 trade union headquarters and they had
destroyed 200 socialist centres. Admittedly they had suffered
losses of their own.

Meanwhile he was promising everybody everything; and one by
one he contradicted all his former views. Don Sturzo, leader of the
Catholic-inspired Popular Party pointed out his inconsistencies:

Don Sturzo He was an anti-militarist, opposed to colonial enterprise,
denying the duty of defending his country, and he became an
interventionist with imperialist tendencies. His mind, given to
excessive simplification, is bound to no formula; he can pass from
theory to theory, from position to position, rapidly, even incon-
sistently, with neither remorse nor regret.

Professor Sammy Finer At this point the Prime Minister, the aged
Giolitti, called yet another election. He was negotiating with
Mussolini for some time. He now offered the Fascist Party a place
in his own governmental election bloc. Mussolini now moved on

to this alternative, this legalistic strategy. He accepted Giolitti's offer. In the election he won a seat and his party won another thirty four. But it was only a modest toehold, and once in parliament Mussolini began to realise that the tide of public opinion was now swinging away from the violence of his brutal lieutenants in the provinces.

He decided to call a halt and play the parliamentary game. He therefore concluded a peace pact with the socialists; but it was too late. His lieutenants refused to comply and since he now insisted, they actually expelled him from his own party! He was brought back only by a compromise. He would not publicly denounce the pact, but he would not restrain the fascist *squadristi* either. And so the violence continued.

And now the Fascist movement began to move in upon, to occupy and take over the local government in one after another of the cities of the north. The Socialist Party had now split into two factions. The unions were getting feebler. They made their last great effort in July 1921; they called a general strike. The fascist squads broke it and the socialist movement was defeated. In their newspaper, *Jiustizia* on 12 August 1922, they admitted their demoralisation.

Jiustizia Every important centre bears the marks of the Fascist hurricane. We must face facts: the Fascists are masters of the field. Nothing is to prevent them dealing more heavy blows in the certainty of winning fresh victories.

Professor Sammy Finer By now, all that remained between Mussolini and power was the government in Rome. But in Rome, the parliamentary system was in its death throes. It was capable of only ineffectual manoeuvres. Pietro Nenni, a life-long socialist and former colleague of Mussolini, has left this vivid description.

Pietro Nenni With but a few exceptions the ruling class in Italy was morally decadent. It entirely failed to realise the perils threatening the country. Its mediocrity was such that it was incapable of rising above its petty quarrels and personal jealousies to a general view of the crisis. The country demanded a man at the head of the government, and all it could offer was a grotesque and ridiculous puppet in the person of Signor Facta, a moral and physical caricature of authority. Wait and see – such was the programme of a majority which had no sense of its obligation, had no ideals and was staggering along the road to its last and definite defeat.

Professor Sammy Finer But thou gh Mussolini did not fear these politicians, he did fear the arm y. Only two years before, he had seen it drive the Black-Shirted legions of the Poet D'Annunzio from the town of Fiume which t hey had illegally occupied. Mussolini well knew that his militia men were no match for the regulars. And so he played a double game. He negotiated with politicians in Rome for a part in a coalition government. But he also laid plans with his lieutenants for one final act of intimidation. The squads would move from the cities they had occupied and they would now converge to threaten the capital city itself.

When the Fascist Congress met in Naples in October 1922, Mussolini shouted:

Benito Mussolini What we have in view is the introduction into the liberal state of all the forces of a new generation which has emerged from the war and the vict ory. Either the government will be given to us or we shall seize it by marching on Rome.

Professor Sammy Finer And so, on the night of 27 October, columns of Fascists began to converge on Rome. Mussolini however remained prudently behind in Milan which is very near indeed to the Swiss frontier, in case the bluff miscarried. And it very nearly did. A mere 12,000 men moved on Rome. They were wretchedly armed. They bivouacked in the soaking torrential autumn rain. And while they did so, the aged Prime Minister Facta decided to declare a state of siege and call out the troops against them.

There is no question but that the Rome garrison would have dispersed with ease this ill-armed sodden rabble. But Mussolini had not temporised in vain. His political opponents were less resolute than even he had calculated. For when the Prime Minister took the martial law decree to the King on the 28th, the King refused to sign. Instead the Prime Minister was empowered to offer the Fascists a place in a Cabinet. But it was too late. Mussolini's demands had risen as he sensed his opponents' weakness. Now he demanded the Prime Ministership for himself.

Benito Mussolini This is the situation. The greater part of northern Italy is in the hands of the Fascists. Central Italy – Tuscany, Umbria, the Marches, Alto Lazio – is occupied by the Blackshirts. Where the police headquarters and the prefectures have not been taken by assault, the Fascists have occupied stations and post offices, which are the nerve centres of the nation.

A tremendous victory is in sight, with the almost unanimous approval of the nation. But victory is not to be mutilated by eleventh hour combinations. It was really not worth the trouble mobilising merely in order to reach a deal with Salandra. The Government must have a clear Fascist character.

Fascism will not abuse its victory, but is determined that it shall not be diminished. Let that be clear to all. Fascism wants power and will have it.

Professor Sammy Finer The next day a telegram arrived asking Mussolini to come to Rome in order to become Prime Minister. The rain-sodden Fascist bands were hurriedly moved into Rome to greet his arrival.

So, as Mussolini had said – Fascism had wanted power and Fascism was going to have it. And now Fascism – or rather Mussolini – had got it. And once he was Prime Minister, on 29 October 1922, he began to consolidate his hold on the nation; progressively he abolished all constitutional restraints, he dissolved all hostile associations and parties and turned his rule into a personal dictatorship which endured until in 1943, the entire edifice collapsed under the weight of military defeat.

What was this Fascism that had wanted power and won it? Was it not rather Mussolini than a doctrine called Fascism? In the last months of his life Mussolini provided his own answer. This is what he told Pavolini, his latest and his last party boss.

Benito Mussolini Fascism is Mussolinism. Let us not delude ourselves. As a doctrine Fascism contains nothing new; it is a product of a modern crisis, the crisis of man who can no longer remain within the normal bounds of life with its conventionalism, within the bounds of the existing human laws. I would call it irrationalism.

There is such a thing as morality, but we're tired of it; and I'd go further and say that it makes no impression on us.

We are tormented people; everyone of us would like to be in the sun, the pole of life for himself and for others. There you have the evil at the heart of the modern man; call it irrationalism, Bolshevism, Fascism. Let us consider that last term: what would Fascism be, if I had not been?

5 Pandit Nehru
1889-1964

Interim Prime Minister before Independence 1946–7
Prime Minister of India 1947-64

Professor W. H. Morris-Jones When Jawaharlal Nehru died in 1964, he
had been Prime Minister of India for seventeen years and people
spoke of 'the Nehru era' having ended. He had been for most of that
period in virtual control of the destinies of 500 million people, one
in six of the human race, and he had also been for much of the time
the acknowledged leader of the third world of new states. When
the British wound up their empire in India in 1947, power was
transferred, and chiefly it was Nehru's hands that received it. In
mid-August of that year Lord Mountbatten, the last Viceroy, laid
down the century-old imperial power and Nehru it was who
announced the birth of the new India.

Jawaharlal Nehru Long years ago we made a tryst with destiny, and
now the time comes when we shall redeem our pledge, not wholly
or in full measure, but very substantially. At the stroke of the
midnight hour, when the world sleeps, India will awake to life and
freedom.

Professor W. H. Morris-Jones India's tryst with destiny – this wasn't
just a change of government such as brought a Baldwin or a
Roosevelt to power, it was not even a change of régime within a
nation as when Mussolini seized the Italian state. This was one
people taking over from the imperial grasp of another different and
distant people. But was there also a personal Nehru tryst with
destiny? What kind of man was this who succeeded to the throne
of Delhi? And how had he got there?

Lord Brockway, perhaps better known as Fenner Brockway and
a lifelong friend of Nehru, remembers first meeting him in England
in 1911 when he was a young man of twenty-two.

Lord Brockway I went to the Cambridge University Labour Club to
speak on Imperialism. Nehru had been there but he was then a

student of law in London. But he'd come to Cambridge for the weekend and I had coffee with him afterwards. He was slight, very well-dressed, well-mannered, almost European. I was interested to find that he thought my speech was extremist. I had been urging that India should move on to independence and he did not have then either extreme nationalist views or even a beginning of his socialist views.

Professor W. H. Morris-Jones That was evidently a very quiet beginning. But Nehru was a quiet man, at least that was one aspect of his personality. I met him several times during that momentous year of 1947 and he struck me as fundamentally very reserved, even withdrawn at times, preoccupied with his own thoughts, inclined to worry. And yet this is the same man who could capture and move great crowds. That's one paradox – this solitary individualist who relished and needed face-to-face contact with the masses.

But there are other contradictions in his personality too. The Nehru outbursts of temper were famous and there were several occasions when his anger would show in physical violence: disorderly crowds made him mad and he would stride in and lay about him. This fits in oddly with the other picture, equally true, of the soft-spoken, rather cautious and diffident man, almost donnish in manner. It was this side that impressed Ian Stephens, former editor of the Calcutta *Statesman*, when he met Nehru in the summer of 1931.

Ian Stephens I was introduced by this colleague of mine, but I didn't catch the name and it was very curious. I felt quite rapidly, within a matter of seconds of talking to this man, as if I was back in Cambridge, talking to a young Cambridge don. It was delightful, but it was odd.

And whether I realised later on in the conversation or only afterwards that this man was Nehru, I don't know, but that was my first impression of Nehru, of something palely brown in complexion, but extremely English and Cambridgey in manner, accent and method of thought.

Professor W. H. Morris-Jones Nehru was a man of ideas, not an original thinker, but perfectly at home discussing general notions. This gave him an advantage and perhaps a sense of superiority over his colleagues in the nationalist movement. Combined with his education

– natural sciences at Cambridge and law in London – and also, most important in India, his distinguished family background, this led some to see in him a kind of double arrogance.

Ian Stephens Certainly from subsequent meetings I would say he was an arrogant man, arrogant perhaps from patrician causes, aristocratic causes, and arrogant also intellectually, I'd say, the arrogance of the doctrinaire.

Professor W. H. Morris-Jones Nehru himself wondered if his arrogance disqualified him from political leadership. In 1937 he wrote anonymously a strange portrait of himself.

Jawaharlal Nehru Watch his smiles as he addresses the crowds. Is all this natural, or the carefully thought out trickery of the public man? Perhaps it is both. Steadily and persistently he goes on increasing his personal prestige and influence. . . . From the far North to Cape Cormorin he has gone like some triumphant Caesar, leaving a trail of glory and legend behind him. Is all this just a passing fancy which amuses him – or is it his will to power that is driving him from crowd to crowd? . . . What if the fancy turns?

Men like Jawaharlal are unsafe in a democracy. He calls himself a democrat and a socialist, and no doubt he does so in all earnestness; but a little twist and he might turn into a dictator. . . . Jawaharlal cannot become a fascist . . . he is too much of an aristocrat for the crudity and vulgarity of fascism. And yet he has all the makings of a dictator in him – vast popularity, a strong will, energy, pride – and with all his love of the crowd, an intolerance of others and a certain contempt for the weak and inefficient. His flashes of temper are well known. His conceit is already formidable. It must be checked. We want no Caesars.

Professor W. H. Morris-Jones But this proud and dreamy doctrinaire is not the whole truth either. Nehru was also a great man for reconciling opposites, securing cooperation, and he showed very amply, especially later on, that he had an extraordinary energy and capacity for pretty humdrum organising and administrative work.

So the paradoxes multiply, and I am tempted to think that this is not a peculiarity of Nehru but something common to most political leaders. Complexity of personality is almost a necessary qualification for rising to the top of the power ladder; the exercise of power calls for very diverse attributes, even contradictory qualities.

In Nehru's case, it's fascinating that the man himself was so sharply aware of his mixed nature. He worried especially and indeed wrote about how far someone as westernised as he was could ever be a genuine Indian leader.

Jawahalal Nehru Indeed, I often wonder if I represent anyone at all, and I am inclined to think that I do not, though many have kindly and friendly feelings towards me. I have become a queer mixture of the East and the West, out of place everywhere, at home nowhere.

I cannot get rid of either that past inheritance or my recent acquisitions. They are both part of me, and though they help me in both the East and the West, they also create in me a feeling of spiritual loneliness not only in public activities but in life itself. I am a stranger and alien in the West. I cannot be of it. But in my own country also, sometimes, I have an exile's feeling.

Professor W. H. Morris-Jones So there is a puzzle. This is not a frustrated man with a grudge against society, trying to compensate by thrusting towards great power, rather it's an uneasy man striving to become a good Indian instead of an exile. And the question is just how, by what route, did this man climb to the peak of power?

There are certain ways in which it is quite clear that Nehru was 'born great' – I mean that fortune favoured him with a good start. For one thing he was born about the right time. When the British were ready to hand over in 1947, Nehru was fifty-eight, old enough to be well-known and well-established, but not so old, as perhaps Gandhi was by then, as to be weary. He was in his political prime at the right moment.

Nehru was also born in the right part of India – in the Hindi heartland of the subcontinent. It would have been just that bit more difficult to have become an all-India leader if he hailed from one of the circumference regions such as Madras.

Above all, Nehru came from a family of status. The Nehrus were Brahmins, Kashmiri Brahmins, cream of the cream. It was at the same time a thrusting, modernising family, part of the wealthy professional class. It not only bought him English education, it gave him from childhood the feel of public life, the confidence of belonging to an élite, the assurance that he would someday be someone. Lord Brockway puts the point succinctly when talking about the young Nehru.

Lord Brockway After all, he was born with a political spoon in his mouth. His father was Motilal Nehru, the rich, very celebrated lawyer, and the whole atmosphere of his home was politics, and I think, undoubtedly, he intended to become a political figure even then.

Professor W. H. Morris-Jones But it is seldom enough to be favoured by birth. And if Nehru was born great it's equally clear that he is also among those who have greatness thrust upon them. One man above all others was in a position to make or break Nehru's political career: that man was Gandhi and he chose to make Nehru. Nehru spoke of Gandhi with the utmost of respect and affection.

Jawaharlal Nehru In fact it is not easy for me to talk much about Gandhiji. Persons who have influenced one greatly are difficult to deal with. The fact that stood out about Gandhiji was how he attracted people of different kinds, completely different kinds, and thereby he became, you might say, a link between different groups, different individuals, from the poorest peasant, whom he always sought to represent, to princes and rich industrialists and others. They were all attracted in their own way and no doubt influenced by him to some extent.

Some of us were influenced much more, because we actually worked with him, were influenced I suppose ... well I don't know how to define the bigness of an individual. He was certainly the biggest individual that I had come across in my life.

Professor W. H. Morris-Jones Nehru was of course praising in Gandhi the very qualities which later people came to see in Nehru himself.

The strange relationship between these two, absolutely central to the rise of Nehru, began at a crucial moment for both of them. Gandhi had returned from South Africa and made his appearance on the Indian political scene. He wanted to mobilise India against imperial rule and he found the existing methods inadequate. Terrorism was futile and sedate constitutional protest seemed ineffective. In the techniques of civil disobedience and non-cooperation – what Gandhi called *satyagraha* – he believed that he had found the key, a way of getting mass action involving disciplined organisation and political education, while at the same time not using violence or inviting violence.

But Gandhi needed converts – he had to win over a number of the established political leaders like Nehru's father, and he had to recruit also a band of youthful devotees of whom the younger Nehru was one of the first. From his side too, Nehru needed Gandhi. Nehru had returned from England, but had not been able to settle purposefully. He began to practise law, he made his first timid steps in public life, but nothing really excited him until he heard Gandhi's disobedience call in 1921. Then almost overnight, the bored dilettante was turned into a crusading soldier.

Within months Nehru was in prison, serving the first of his nine terms – he was imprisoned by the British for his political activities for a total of nine years. There was to be no real going back on this close tie with Gandhi. For the young Nehru, Gandhi became teacher, second father and most intimate friend. Datta Tahmankar a writer and journalist who knew Nehru very well for most of his political career, bears witness to this closeness:

Datta Tahmankar As their relationship developed, it ceased to be merely that of *guru* and disciple – *guru*, that is teacher, holy teacher, and, his disciple – but they became real friends, attached to each other emotionally, which proved of immense importance in the development of Nehru and also in the political development of India.

Professor W. H. Morris-Jones This intimacy is confirmed by Lord Brockway, but he also points to their political differences:

Lord Brockway I should have said that at this stage he came very much under the magnetism of Gandhi, but I was interested to find that whilst he had this personal devotion to him, he still did have his political doubts.

Professor W. H. Morris-Jones Political doubts were not surprising. Many must have wondered what there could be in common between the sophisticated Nehru, eager for modernisation, drawn to socialist ideas, and the older man, a spiritual as much as a political leader. Ian Stephens underlines this contrast.

Ian Stephens After all, Gandhi was some sort of a saint. He was a deeply religious man, a man of anachronistic crankiness and fads, a spinning wheel and all this sort of thing, back to the villages. It was very different indeed to Nehru's outlook as an agnostic and a westernised person, impressed by the importance of industry and so on.

Professor W. H. Morris-Jones Gandhi and Nehru were really like two lovers. There were stormy moments in their relations, but they simply could not bear to part. The storms usually came because Gandhi would suddenly do something unexpected and even eccentric, quite exasperating to Nehru.

In the very first disobedience movement, Gandhi abruptly called it off just when it was getting up steam. Why? Because of one isolated incident of violence, and Nehru exploded: 'Must we train the millions of India in the theory and practice of non-violence before we can go forward?' But then he quickly reminded himself, 'Without Gandhi, where is our movement?'

Or again in the later movement in 1932, Gandhi signs a truce with the British and then undertakes a fast to prevent the untouchables from being split off from the main electorate through a separate franchise. Another Nehru explosion – why on earth sidetrack the movement on to minor issues in this irresponsible way? His feeling that the old man was impossible was enhanced when Gandhi followed up that fast with another, one that had no overt political goal at all, aimed, as he put it, at self-purification. What sort of political leadership was this? In despair, Nehru sent Gandhi a telegram: 'What can I say about matters I do not understand? I feel lost in a strange country', and then adds, 'where you are the only landmark'. A couple of hours later, upset at having sent that wire to a man who was after all risking death through fasting, he sent another saying, 'Whatever happens, it is well, and whatever happens, you win'.

That's the point indeed. Gandhi always seemed to win, to have his way, and always it was Nehru who had to make the concessions. He did so out of personal affection and respect, but also because in his view to desert Gandhi would be to weaken the national movement. But whatever the reasons – and one can find no one willing to suggest that Nehru was acting out of an opportunist desire to curry favour – the result was that Gandhi comes to think of Nehru as his real successor. Lord Brockway believes this was clear quite early on.

Lord Brockway Undoubtedly by 1928, Gandhi regarded Jawaharlal Nehru as his successor. I don't think there was any real doubt.

Professor W. H. Morris-Jones Not everyone agrees on this. Ian Stephens, for example, takes a different view.

Ian Stephens I don't think that anyone in the 1930s would have said that

Nehru was the undisputed number two. He was one of, one might say, a dozen leading Congressmen who had their own provincial, local followings and who were in and out of various party offices of the Congress Party.

Professor W. H. Morris-Jones Be that as it may, it is easy to spot the three key moments when Gandhi pushes Nehru forward. And each time it's a question of nomination to the office of party president.

First, in 1929 – Nehru had been away on a long visit to Europe and had returned filled with radical and socialist ideas. Gandhi wrote to him, 'You are going too fast . . . encouraging mischief-makers and hooligans', and Gandhi feared that they might have to part political company, as Nehru stormed furiously around the country. But what Gandhi did was to back the thirtynine-year-old Nehru against a more senior rival, Patel. Was Gandhi aiming to tame the wild radical or to test him for the future? The answer is both – and at the same time also save the movement from being deserted by the impatient young. Gandhi defended his choice of Nehru by saying, 'Who can excel him in love of the country? If he has the dash and rashness of the warrior he has also the prudence of the statesman. He will not force the pace to breaking point.'

On the second occasion, 1936, the situation in the movement was critical, a left-right split threatened; and again Gandhi steers Nehru into the leadership for a two-year spell. Party unity is saved even if the left is somewhat let down by Nehru. Patel is again put on one side.

And when this happened for the final time, in 1946, so that it was Nehru who saw through the negotiations to independence, no one should really have been surprised. Because in 1940 Gandhi had already made the succession position clear. 'We have had our differences . . . and yet I have said and say again that Jawaharlal will be my successor . . . I know this, that when I am gone he will speak my language.' With all this prompting and helping from Gandhi, was Nehru's way to the top then perfectly plain sailing and easy?

Lord Brockway I should have said so – I should have said it was almost inevitable. I mean first his family background, secondly his close association with Gandhi, third his ability to rally to Gandhi certain sections of the Indian people. He was a coalescing personal influence.

Professor W. H. Morris-Jones Being born great and having greatness thrust upon him are all very well, but we must also see Nehru as having achieved greatness, achieved it by very special qualities and very hard work. After all Gandhi was an exacting judge and a shrewd one. To pass out first from his examination was itself a summary of achievements.

Gandhi had seen that Nehru had the dynamism and unflagging energy of a campaigner. He had adequately tested his loyalty to the cause, his patriotism. He had also seen that for all his reserve and his sophistication, Nehru was willing to slog it out in party committees, doing the drudgery of political organiser. Nehru had also given enough evidence of his persuasiveness, his willingness to compromise, to suggest that he could hold diverse elements together.

Above all, Gandhi had seen and valued Nehru's vast popularity with younger people and with radical elements. And behind that popularity was his personal charm and warmth and sincerity.

Datta Tahmankar His sincerity was such that it could come out transparently when he spoke to the villagers. They might not understand what he was saying – higher politics of international affairs and things like that – but there was a man who was utterly sincere and they felt he was one of them.

Professor W. H. Morris-Jones And Krishna Menon, who knew Nehru from the thirties, and as Defence Minister was a cabinet colleague with him in the later years, endorses the importance of his personal qualities:

Krishna Menon I don't think we should discount or even underestimate the role of his personality and personal character. I think it is true to say that every person thought he had a personal relation with him. They felt Nehru was concerned about them. The people had a feeling that he was concerned about their business as such. He was interested in the well-being of India. The masses were India to him and he knew that the power of India lay in those masses and he sought to find them.

After he came back from England, very much an educated upper class kind of person, he went out and for a year he wandered among the peasants and he would understand them. He said, 'They looked into my eyes and I looked into theirs.'

And then he tried to, as far as he could – and I think successfully to a great extent – translate the abstruse principles of higher ideals into the terms of the people as such, not by sending them to school, but by his way and power of speaking. He was a man whom we can call a great mass educator. His speeches were not set speeches of short duration – sometimes they were long. Especially in later years, they covered all sorts of subjects – maybe atomic energy, maybe a scientific approach to life, maybe the caste system, maybe social evils, maybe international affairs. In a speech he covered the whole of those fields. It is not because he was rambling around but because this was the only way of educating a country of over 300 million people. You can't send them all to school. And our elections and our campaigns were great campaigns of mass education – even now to a certain extent they remain so.

Professor W. H. Morris-Jones So the picture begins to come together – the elements of initial advantages, of personal qualities and those helpful pushes forward. But there's no simple inevitability about this. At several points Nehru could have taken decisions that might have put him out of the running.

If he had followed his radicalism and struck out on his own, if he had been too impatient to bother with the conservative Gandhians, if he had responded to the pressing invitations to lead the left, any of these courses could have led to the wilderness. But Nehru's temperament kept him close to the mainstream.

It is not the cunning of the person that accounts for his emergence at the top. Rather it's what Hegel called the cunning in history, the conspiracy of events in conjunction. In a sense the proof of the pudding is available: if it had been a fluke, a stray chance, would Nehru, alone of all the leaders of the new states, have been able to survive all the seventeen years?

Fortune undoubtedly played its part with Nehru, but a man who could dominate for two decades needs more than luck – he needed and had qualities which matched the needs, or met the demands of the situation. This is what took him to the top and enabled him to stay there.

6 Kwame Nkrumah

1909-

Leader of Government Business, Gold Coast 1951-2
Prime Minister before Independence 1952-7
Prime Minister of Ghana 1957-60
President 1960-6

Kwame Nkrumah At long last the battle has ended. Ghana, your beloved
country is free for ever. From now on, today, we must change our
attitudes, our minds. We must realise that from now on we are no
more a colonial, but a free and independent people

Dr Richard Rathbone Kwame Nkrumah, Ghana's first Prime Minister
and later her first President, celebrating her independence from
British rule in 1957. After this date most black African states were
to be ushered into independence with similar speeches but this was
the first. Much of Nkrumah's reputation lies in his collection of
firsts. Because of this above all he was a significant figure for all
African nationalists, a symbol of what could be done, as well as
something of a bogeyman for colonial governments. He was and
probably still remains the best-known nationalist name inside
Africa and outside, despite his fall from power in 1966.

We have little on his very early life other than his own account.
Two important factors about his birth are apparent. Firstly his
birth in 1909 was humble; he was the son of one of the several
wives of a poor south-western craftsman. He was to use his origins
skilfully throughout his career; he was a man of the people, not
much different from those he was to lead.

Secondly he was born conveniently into a branch of the dominant
linguistic and cultural group of Ghana. Any national leader in
Ghana derives advantages from being identified with the majority
cultural group. But before these advantages became politically
significant, at school they were embarrassments.

Not at the Roman Catholic Elementary school at Half Assini,
where he started his education. It was there he'd been helped by a
priest, George Fischer, who'd spotted his abilities and got him in to
Achimota College, the élite secondary school of the Gold Coast. It

was 1926 and Kwame Nkrumah was seventeen. But at Achimota, his humble rural background was a disadvantage, as his old schoolmaster, the Rev. Sandy Fraser, emphasises here.

Rev. Sandy Fraser He didn't think that his contemporaries in Achimota had any regard or respect for him and they wrote him off because of his tribe and background. I think he overcame that largely under the influence of Aggrey.

Dr Richard Rathbone Sandy Fraser emphasises here the influence of the great African educationalist, Kweggir Aggrey, upon Nkrumah. It was Aggrey who had persuaded the reforming Governor Guggisberg to build at Achimota one of the best secondary schools in Africa and then Aggrey proceeded to teach there.

Nkrumah's initial unhappiness didn't last very long, however, and he settled down, eventually becoming a prefect and very good athlete, and a leading light in the debating society. Nkrumah's teachers were more impressed by his tenacity and loquacity than by his intellectual ability.

Rev. Sandy Fraser He wasn't outstandingly able, I would say. He was outstandingly talkative. I remember that I had to take over the history class that Dr Aggrey had taken, of which Kwame Nkrumah was one. I had to give a general background of Africa as a start, you know, with the Gold Coast setting in Africa and I spoke about the Tuaregs and Arabs in the North and the Pigmies and Hottentots and so on, and suddenly Kwame interrupted and said, 'I don't agree with a word you are saying. Dr Aggrey told us that all Africans are one. We are one people from North to South'.

And I said, 'Well, there are great differences – there are great differences in tradition, there are differences even in physique and appearance'.

'No, I can't accept that.'

And I said, 'Oh, shut up.' I said, 'We will talk about it afterwards'.

Well, we spoke about it after the lesson and he was really fiercely angry that Dr Aggrey's statements should be called in question, as he thought, and he said, 'Well, I'll never accept what you say'.

Well, that was fairly typical of the man, and yet he didn't bear a grudge. I mean, once you had listened to all he had to say fairly patiently and still disagreed with him, he would agree to differ.

Dr Richard Rathbone One can see there not only his loyalty to Dr Aggrey, but a very early commitment to Aggrey's Pan-African ideals, which Nkrumah later was to develop himself, and indeed become the prime exponent of in Africa.

Was this also the period when his Ghanaian nationalist views were beginning to crystallise? Sandy Fraser thinks it was.

Rev. Sandy Fraser I think this was the start of a nationalist orientation to all his thinking. At that stage he already had an idea of an independent Gold Coast. As a matter of fact everybody at Achimota realised that this was an ideal for which we must work. But he did see himself as directly involved, and this was what he was determined to make the aim and object of his life. Yes, I think it is quite true to say that he was a nationalist from his second year at Achimota onwards.

Dr Richard Rathbone Nkrumah graduated from Achimota in 1930 and took up teaching posts in Catholic junior schools. By the age of twenty-five, despite his nationalist leanings, he had done little more than found a teachers' association at Elmina which appears to have been markedly unradical.

But the reasons for his growing anti-colonialism are clear. Rural, poor and owing what status he had to educational success rather than high birth, Nkrumah was very much one of a new generation who suffered particularly from inequalities arising out of the colonial situation, uneven distribution of resources, political impotence, paternalism. Most importantly, they were a generation who were to use political protest in an entirely new way. They were educated and so saw the futility of isolated violence or traditional methods of protest. Nkrumah's appeal was to be to this, his peer-group, and not to ethnic sensitivities, traditional values, or limited class objectives.

But ironically, as the pace of protest increased, Nkrumah left the Gold Coast in 1935, not to return again until 1947. He went to America in search of higher education, America, because he had failed his London matriculation in Latin and mathematics, and America because he had influential connections with a Negro college, Lincoln, which gave him a place. Sandy Fraser feels that the decision to go to America was partly political:

Rev. Sandy Fraser When he left Achimota he took up a teaching job with the Roman Catholics and then he got a scholarship to America and I am sure that he took this scholarship and was delighted to get it because he felt that this was going to fit him to be a national leader.

Dr Richard Rathbone Lincoln was no picnic. Despite the scholarship, Nkrumah had to work in a ship-yard, a soap-factory and at dish-washing as well as the more usual American customs of serving at table in the University dining hall, and working as a library assis-tant.

But it was also a time of political awakening and activity. Nkrumah wrote this about his American days.

Kwame Nkrumah I made time to acquaint myself with as many political organisations in the United States as I could. These included the Republicans, the Democrats, the Communists and the Trotskyites. My aim was to learn the technique of organisation. I knew that when I eventually returned to the Gold Coast, I was going to be faced with this problem. I knew that whatever the programme for the solution of the colonial question might be, success would de-pend upon the organisation adopted.

Dr Richard Rathbone There is hindsight at work here all right, but one can cut through much of it. The picture that Nkrumah offers of himself, the schemer, the long-term planner, the patient revolu-tionary is almost certainly overdramatic. But it was surely a period of great change for him. He was becoming a committed radical politician, perhaps because education had provided him with logical ways of ordering what he might have felt before, but could not articulate. From his writing of the period it is clear that he had been reading books to which it was unlikely that he had even had access in the Gold Coast.

After ten years in America he arrived in London in May 1945, with degrees in economics and sociology and, perhaps more surprisingly, theology. He was to work on philosophy at University College, London, politics at the LSE, and keeping options open, he also enrolled at Grays Inn. But the activity was now almost com-pletely political.

Sam Morris, a West Indian journalist who knew Nkrumah well in those days, describes their first meeting.

Sam Morris I would have met him at the home of George Padmore.

Padmore's home in Cranleigh Street at the time was a sort of Mecca for all the African students and would-be leaders who thought along the lines that Padmore did. But at that time I was secretary of the League of Coloured Peoples and I met Africans from all over the world, from all over the African continent, and I must say that there was nothing spectacular at that time which impressed me about Kwame Nkrumah.

Dr Richard Rathbone Maybe nothing spectacular initially. Nkrumah was after all new to London, and still uncertain of himself. But it is significant that he steered straight into the small but vibrant coterie of anti-imperialists led by George Padmore, the West Indian radical leader.

Padmore was another in the line of Nkrumah's father-figures. These had started with Fischer, Aggrey and Fraser in his school-days, went on to his tutor Dr Johnson at Lincoln, and continued in London with Padmore.

The circumscribed world of black student politics in London was the spawning ground of many nationalist leaders. For Nkrumah it was a period of rich experience. There was the hectic round of meetings, haranguing at Hyde Park, heckling imperialist politicians. He was befriended by the anti-colonial sympathisers in British politics, the Fabians as well as the British Communist Party, and he made his mark on them.

In looking at the brief London period one is struck for the first time by the organisational ability and the energy. He was on endless committees and not always the powerless idealistic may-fly organisations, but the kind of committee that could bring two hundred delegates from Africa, the United States and the West Indies to Manchester for the 6th Pan-African Congress of 1945. It was a meeting of historical importance and for Nkrumah it heralded arrival on the international scene.

But despite his role as joint organising secretary of the Manchester Congress, Sam Morris feels Nkrumah had not yet reached his organisational peak.

Sam Morris I don't know if his skill as an organiser was as highly developed in this country as it was later. It wasn't of course, because he hadn't the material anyway. Many a time he could hardly get the money to pay his rent in the Grays Inn Road office, you know. But even under those difficult circumstances he did manage to keep the thing going. But his genius as a real organiser showed itself after he got his own party going and he was back home.

Dr Richard Rathbone Nevertheless one must remember the skills Nkrumah had acquired before returning to the Gold Coast. He had organised a major international congress, he had managed to run on a shoe-string a series of African students organisations, he was a sadder but wiser newspaper proprietor, his *New African* newspaper having landed him in debt in London. He was a pamphleteer, an organiser of demonstrations and by now he was a practised public speaker. There was little he had not dabbled in; he ha acquired a sort of nationalist politician's tool-kit.

But one was not going to achieve independence by preaching to the converted at Hyde Park or in Red Lion Square. Nationalists need nations and Nkrumah had been away for twelve years. In the Gold Coast, outside the charmed circle of political cognoscenti, he was virtually unknown.

In August 1947, the Ghanaian élite nationalists had reformed into a new grouping, the United Gold Coast Convention. Nkrumah was to call them later 'a movement backed almost entirely by reactionaries, middle-class lawyers and merchants'. Ostensibly arguing for self-government in the shortest possible time, they were rather a professional and business lobby demanding a greater slice of the pie, a relaxation of war-time restrictions and a greater share, for themselves, in government. Busy men at the bar and in business, they needed a full-time organising secretary. One of their number, Ako Adjei, who was to become one of Nkrumah's ministers, had known Nkrumah in America. Why not Nkrumah for secretary?

But as they were to find out, non-professional politicians with alternative careers and no real desire to dirty their hands in the hard graft of popular politics are very vulnerable to the ambitions of a full-time secretary.

Nkrumah returned to take up this post at the turn of 1947. The UGCC was concerned to harness the discontent then widespread in the Gold Coast. It wished to use the protest to force the Colonial Government to concede to the Party's programme. But the UGCC was not a mass party and right from the beginning Nkrumah took a much more populist line than they. He had the time, the energy and the ideals to make the propagation of his ideas effective. He extended the Convention's contacts so that inside two months there were something like 500 small branches of the Party, not just in the prosperous south, where most of the intelligentsia came from, but in the remoter areas of the country and amongst remote people. He was obviously more at home amongst people with a similar background to himself than any of his more patrician colleagues on the Convention.

But above all there was his organisational skill. We asked a political colleague of the time, Kwesi Armah, later to become Ghana's High Commissioner in London, how Nkrumah managed to get himself known in Ghana so quickly.

Kwesi Armah By sheer organisation, and by carrying the programme to the people. In point of fact, he put up a proper programme for the first time. Nkrumah was a realist, and Nkrumah was prepared to see a mass movement, to see a situation whereby the life of the ordinary man in the street was bettered.

Dr Richard Rathbone Inevitably, because he was the most dynamic of the group, the new political dynamism of the UGCC became associated in the popular mind with Nkrumah himself.

Kwesi Armah Nkrumah had a great appeal so far as young people were concerned. You see, he was thought of as a very selfless person. Here you are with a man who was prepared to work for nothing, to work gratis for the cause of Ghana to attain independence.

Nkrumah is a very simple man. That is the thing which made a great impact on everybody; he was a very simple man and was able to travel to the various villages to sit down and eat simple meals with people, and this made a great impression on them. He would walk for miles, miles on end, to really propagate a cause and tell them what was happening.

Dr Richard Rathbone From the beginning, most of the leaders of the UGCC resented his success, objected to his radicalism which threatened them as well as the colonial government. And he in turn built up his own political support, although he was still working for the UGCC and being paid for it.

In February 1948 the split broadened when six members of the UGCC, including Nkrumah, were detained as a result of emergency powers taken because of widespread urban rioting. The other leaders hated being in prison but Nkrumah knew its political value. In the months that followed the riots, a commission of enquiry recommended among other things universal suffrage. It also recommended the creation of a committee to work out a new constitution. The UGCC was well represented on this committee, but Nkrumah wasn't. He was excluded because the commission of enquiry had concluded that if he wasn't actually a communist, then he was something very like one.

The UGCC's involvement on the constitutional committee gave them a vested interest in playing down agitational politics. It was clear that the colonial government wanted them to win the future elections. But Nkrumah's hands were free. He could agitate and they could not. The UGCC had been used by him and he slowly split from them, taking with him the youth organisation that he had built up within it. By June 1949, this had become the Convention People's Party, militant, radical and scornful of colonial government, chiefs and the urban intelligentsia. The CPP left the UGCC in limbo without visible means of support. David Williams, the editor of the magazine *West Africa*, describes the impact of this new political party:

David Williams The essence of the Convention People's Party was that it saw that in a country where you have universal suffrage, then one man or one woman's vote is as good as anyone else's. And that was not really the view of the former generation of Ghana politicians, I think, who tended to think – it may have been unconscious – but they tended to think that politics should be the concern of educated and perhaps well-off people, and the masses would be well served by a ruling class who would look after their interests and so forth. But they didn't seriously appeal to the masses.

Dr Richard Rathbone In 1950 Nkrumah was gaoled again, this time for inciting an illegal strike, but his reputation was riding higher than ever. The administration, led by one of Ghana's ablest Governors, Sir Charles Arden-Clarke, soon saw the logic of the situation. Elections were to be held in 1951, and it became clear that the UGCC would not win. The CPP had decided to contest the election as they grew aware of their probable victory. The British government saw its task as moderating the CPP as, like it or not, this was going to be the majority party in the Gold Coast Assembly.

The 1951 elections duly came, the CPP won and Nkrumah was released as an act of grace from imprisonment to become Leader of Government Business. He was at the height of his popularity.

David Williams I think that Kwame Nkrumah deserves credit for the idea that when you have got universal suffrage, then you must appeal to every man and woman throughout the country and not just some middle-class people in the capital city and so on.

I remember somebody in a crowd when he was addressing them saying to me, 'Every man here feels that Kwame is speaking to him, direct, personally'. This was an impression, and that's a marvellous gift.

Dr Richard Rathbone One can see then the accessibility, the charm, the demagogic gifts, and this was a winning combination. Immense personal attraction – charisma perhaps – a new urgent sort of popular politics, a reasonably efficient organisation. It was enough to win three pre-independence elections in 1951, 1954 and 1956 and enough too to convince the British Government that they could not delay independence any longer.

But the charm, the volatility, the reasons why Ghanaians affectionately called him 'show boy', is only one side of the character. Nkrumah had cast off the UGCC with skill and hardness and earned from its rump undying hatred. He was certainly a highly successful political manipulator. Ghanaian politics are tough and he had his tough side.

It is also possible to see in him a desire to please everyone, coupled with the contradictory need to keep the party united and the opposition on the run, and this was a contradiction which he just could not resolve. Sandy Fraser suggests why he couldn't.

Rev. Sandy Fraser I don't think he was ever really able to grasp intellectually the implications of the studies in sociology and philosophy and politics that he undertook. And I don't think he was really able to put in perspective the kind of advice that was offered to him, and that is why he was very much in the hands of whoever happened to be his ministers at any particular time. He never doubted where he wanted to go, but he was a very poor judge, in my opinion, of how to get there. And there is no doubt that all the flattery he received turned his head. He began to think that he had an intuitive grasp of essentials that he simply didn't possess.

Dr Richard Rathbone David Williams feels that, initially at any rate, Nkrumah was aware of his own weaknesses.

David Williams He was a rather ingenuous, modest, slightly frightened man when he was first placed in power, and it took him a long time to believe that he really was in power. I mean he was more surprised than anybody to find that it had come true, and he leant heavily on the British Governor and British Civil Servants, and indeed lots of non-CPP people. What he wanted was help in running the Government, because he knew he couldn't do it.

Dr Richard Rathbone If Nkrumah couldn't really cope with the problems of highest office as Sandy Fraser and David Williams suggest, can his fifteen years in power be explained merely by luck? Certainly there was luck for his nationalist movement. Nkrumah emerged just as the British colonial power was becoming more acquiescent, more prepared to recognise the inevitability of colonial independence.

The CPP was also fortunate in its liberal support from the colonial government, and in particular the personal support Sir Charles Arden-Clarke afforded Nkrumah. Lastly the period up to independence was crowned by record revenue from cocoa, Ghana's main export crop.

But against this, Nkrumah presided very acutely over a turbulent party in which everybody wanted the fruits of independence and power, and for a time he achieved a high degree of national political success. But success over long periods is not always good for political parties and the quality of their leadership.

Kwesi Armah Certainly the party became complacent. The whole party – not Nkrumah – the whole party became complacent at a later stage when Ghana became a one-party democracy and national conferences were not held. In this respect, I would say that we were all very complacent indeed.

Dr Richard Rathbone Many would say that the party leaders were more than just complacent. They had created in Ghana perhaps the best welfare state in Africa, but ironically Ghana was becoming politically more repressive and ruthless in its treatment of the opposition. As for the party itself, David Williams believes that after a time, it actually ceased to exist.

David Williams I don't think anybody actually challenged his leadership, but of course by the end the party didn't exist. I mean, I don't know when they last had a party congress, but there wasn't really any party, it was a fake. At one time there certainly was. The CPP was a very active affair with branches all over the country, which met and campaigned in elections and so on. But slowly he killed the party, I think because it may have produced some rivals to him; but it was not allowed to do so.

Dr Richard Rathbone The reasons behind this ossification of the party were not only political complacency. There was Nkrumah's personal insecurity. Sandy Fraser remembers visiting him in Flagstaff House in Accra in 1964.

Rev. Sandy Fraser I was taken first of all to the private secretary who passed me on to the head of the security, who spoke through an intercom to Kwame who was in a private sanctum; and when Kwame said he was expecting me, the head of security, a colonel, pressed a button and a section of the wall revolved and I went through. It was just like something out of a James Bond novel. And then when I got inside, the wall closed again and there I was in his sanctuary, which was air conditioned and artificially lighted – it had no windows and we were alone together.

I said to Kwame, 'My God', I said, 'you are a bird in a gilded cage, aren't you?'

And Kwame said 'Yes, it's not because I am afraid of my people, it's because my advisers consider these precautions necessary'. Of course, by that time he was actually afraid of his people.

Dr Richard Rathbone Afraid of his people? Well, with every reason; by then there had been at least two serious attempts on his life, one of which had injured him seriously. But justified or not, the divorce from the people, those who had given him and his party life, was almost total towards the end. In increasing isolation, he became more than ever dependent on the advice of others.

The remoteness from the domestic scene, indicated by a greater involvement in extra-Ghanaian affairs undermined his greatest personal and political advantages.

David Williams The man locked up in Flagstaff House, surrounded by guards and so forth, was, I am sure, a different man from the one that I knew before independence, whose main weakness I thought was, first of all, lack of sufficient intelligence always to appreciate the problems with which his government was dealing, and secondly a weakness of character, which allowed him to be too easily swayed by other people.

His strength was that he really and genuinely felt that no Ghanaian was unimportant, wherever he came from, and that every Ghanaian had a right to see him, which was a totally new idea, I think, and made him genuinely very popular for a period.

Dr Richard Rathbone In February 1966 Kwame Nkrumah was ousted along with his party by an army coup d'état. Ghana's new Head of State, General Ankrah, broadcast a message to the people of Ghana.

General Ankrah The National Liberation Council has been established to run the affairs of this country until true democracy, based on the popular will of the people and not on the will of one man alone, has been fully restored to this country.

Dr Richard Rathbone Despite his overthrow Nkrumah's abilities ring clear. From such a humble background to such high office without wear and tear is unthinkable. But he was, as we have heard, kind, energetic, possessed of great stamina, organisational flair, political abilities and personal charm.

Perhaps one might explain the tragic corruption of these estimable qualities in terms of loneliness. At every stage bar the last, when many of his qualities of excellence seemed dim, there was a figure for him to admire and to keep him company. Fischer, Aggrey, Johnson, Padmore, Arden-Clarke – each step higher removed him from the possibility of real friendship. The urge to be liked by all is obvious and the increasing impossibility of intimacy and comfort equally clear.

There is something moving about Sandy Fraser's image of the caged bird, suspicious of nearly everyone, reliant on fawning and on a party machine that made myths about him his own intellect must have rebelled at. The very personal qualities which set him above many in his country also set him apart in an increasingly introspective world of half-truth, delusion and unreality.

7 Sir Winston Churchill
1874-1965

Prime Minister of the U.K.
1940–5, 1951–5

Sir Winston Churchill The whole fury and might of the enemy must very
soon be turned on us. Hitler knows that he will have to break us in
this Island or lose the war. If we can stand up to him, all Europe
may be free and the life of the world may move forward into broad,
sunlit uplands. But if we fail, then the whole world, including
the United States, including all that we have known and cared for,
will sink into the abyss of a new Dark Age, made more sinister,
and perhaps more protracted, by the lights of perverted science.
Let us therefore brace ourselves to our duties, and so bear ourselves
that, if the British Empire and its Commonwealth last for a
thousand years, men will still say: 'This was their finest hour.'

Robert Blake That was Winston Churchill in 1940, just after he had
become Prime Minister, at one of the most crucial moments in the
Second World War. He was twice Prime Minister – 1940 to 1945
and again from 1951 to 1955. But his greatest period is generally
agreed to have been the first. If he had not been Prime Minister in
1940, Britain might not have survived the Second World War.

Yet power came to Churchill very late in life. He was sixty-five –
an age when most people are about to retire. And even so, but for
the war, he might never have climbed to the top. So we are concerned here to discover not how Churchill reached the top eventually but why he did not reach it much earlier. What was it that
kept down the greatest Englishman of the twentieth century while
persons of far inferior calibre governed the country?

Was it due to the envious jealousy of mediocrities who distrusted
genius? Or was it due to defects in his own personality, style and
approach? Or was it a mixture of the two?

To consider what sort of a person he was we must go back to the
beginning. He was born in 1874, the eldest son of Lord Randolph

Churchill, a brilliant but failed politician. He adored his father, but his father regarded him as a fool, apparently with some justification. Sir Harry Verney, later a Liberal M.P. and a member of Asquith's government, was at Harrow with Churchill.

Sir Harry Verney He was a little senior to me, and when I got to Harrow I found there was a well-known tradition of a very stupid little boy who would not learn Latin – nothing would induce him to. And of course we had to start by declining *mensa*, and when we had *mensa*, a table, and then vocative *o mensa*, oh table, Winston went off the deep end. 'I'm not going to learn rubbish like this.' He would not learn any more. I don't think he ever learned the accusative *mensam*. Never got as far as that. And he wouldn't learn and he didn't learn. He was immensely stupid, and known as the most stupid little boy but one in the whole of Harrow. The other, stupidest boy of all was the brother Jack.

I went to Harrow in the early 1890s and he was there – he had been there four years and was still in the lower school. Hadn't learned anything at all, immensely stupid. And they were two immensely stupid little boys and even Weldon couldn't sack two sons of an ex-Chancellor of the Exchequer and so they stayed on and never learned anything at all.

Well then, just at the end of his time at Harrow, suddenly he fell upon English, and Sommervell, Townsend-Warner, Hausen and Bowen taught him the marvels of English. That's what he got out of Harrow at the very end. That's the end of them as far as I am concerned – plenty of stupid little boys, no one as stupid as the two Churchills.

Robert Blake Lord Randolph Churchill died before his son was twenty-one and seems to have regarded him with contempt. Lady Randolph was extravagant and selfish. Winston had an unhappy, unloved childhood. But, whether or not this was the reason, he was from the start intensely ambitious. Mrs Lucy Masterman, widow of C. F. G. Masterman, who was Under-Secretary for Home Affairs when Churchill was Home Secretary, considers that it was not simply ambition.

Mrs C. F. G. Masterman I should put it the opposite way. I think he was terribly afraid of failing. He'd seen his father go down, and he'd read of his father going down like a spent rocket and he

was terribly afraid that he might do the same, I think. I think he
had that sort of fear very strongly – as he once said to my husband,
'I shan't live long', which was a pure delusion – feeling that if he
was to get ahead at all, he must get ahead soon.

Robert Blake Churchill was restless, active and determined to make a
name. His chosen career, to begin with, was the army, and he
contrived to see more campaigning than most cavalry subalterns
managed to experience during those relatively peaceful days – in
Cuba, the North West Frontier of India and in the Sudan.

At the same time he supplemented his income by doing the work
of a war correspondent. He had no resources of his own. He was
anxious to be financially independent before entering politics,
which was always his ultimate purpose; and he made a lot of
money. It was as a special war correspondent that he served in the
South African War and was taken prisoner in November 1899,
escaping a month later. That episode certainly hit the headlines
in a big way.

In the general election of 1900 he got in as Conservative M.P. for
Oldham, and he soon began to attract the attention of the House.
But he did not attract the favour of his leaders. He gained no
promotion from Arthur Balfour, the new Prime Minister.

In 1904, he crossed the floor of the House and became a Liberal.
His public reason was support of free trade against tariffs. Perhaps
it was not his only reason.

Mrs C. F. G. Masterman I do think it was because Balfour treated him
badly. I mean he was far abler than a good many of that front
bench and he was exactly, I should have thought, the sort of young
man who ought to have been hauled in and given the grooming of
an under-secretaryship to teach him the job. But Balfour didn't
like him for some reason, and I think Sandars aggravated the
dislike.

Robert Blake Sandars was Balfour's private secretary and *éminence grise*,
and he perhaps shared Balfour's dislike for Churchill. Churchill, in
an unguarded moment, when asked by Mrs Joseph Chamberlain
why he had crossed the floor, said, 'I know Arthur Balfour will do
nothing for me'.

Whatever his reasons, Churchill's change of party was opportune.
From 1905 for the next seventeen years governments were to be in

power which were either wholly or partly Liberal. Churchill's first office was Colonial Under-Secretary to the Secretary of State, Lord Elgin. Sir Harry Verney, Lord Elgin's private secretary, saw Churchill in action at close range.

Sir Harry Verney Well then, there is Winston as an under-secretary and he couldn't do anything without the approval of the Secretary of State. The Secretary of State was completely dominant. If the Secretary of State said no, it was no, and nothing Winston could do could change it. The troublesome part was when he was going to take notice of places of which he knew nothing. As under-secretary everything went through him, and Winston wrote long minutes in red ink and then these would go up to the Secretary of State. 'E'. That's all – 'E' for Elgin, and that was the end of that file. You couldn't do anything more. You could not appeal. There was nobody to appeal to. You couldn't go beyond that.

If I may be indiscreet, there was one very curious thing that happened; Winston and a governor quarrelled. A very distinguished governor, and Winston wrote to Lord Elgin to say this man must go. 'We must get him to resign.' A long letter in red ink, a page or more. 'No. E.' And over and over again he found his brilliant suggestions 'E', not even 'No', but the particular one on the governor 'No', with the others 'E', 'E', 'E'! We used to look for these to come out. Long long letter from Winston; 'E'! And you couldn't appeal. That was what I think Winston never realised.

But as a matter of fact, of course, Lord Elgin was right and Winston couldn't suddenly think he knew everything and quarrel with governors of whom he knew very little, and he had to be sat on.

But then the next thing Lord Elgin said to me – I was one of his private secretaries – 'We must prevent this man coming dashing into my room without any warning. I am busy talking to a governor or busy doing some very important thing. In comes Winston. I can't have it. You mustn't let him come in'.

So it was given to me to thwart him, and the way I thwarted him was to collect all the people who were faithful, and bring them along the door there, so Winston couldn't get in. And so we did more or less squash Winston and when he wanted to go into Lord Elgin he found the doors blocked. He had to come round by us and get in when he could, in his turn.

Robert Blake This enthusiasm and energy with which Churchill hurled
himself into every job may have been irritating but it was an element
in his rise to power. In 1908 he entered the Cabinet as President of
the Board of Trade and together with Lloyd George as Chancellor
of the Exchequer played an important part in the foundations of
what we now call the welfare state. Two years later Churchill was
made Home Secretary. Lucy Masterman again.

Mrs C. F. G. Masterman Well he was a Home Secretary prepared to do
things. Winston wanted to do things. The head civil servant of
the Home Office once said, 'He drives me crazy sometimes, but he's
the first great Home Secretary we've had since Asquith'.

Robert Blake Mrs Masterman also points out Churchill's considerable
humanity in this most difficult of posts.

Mrs C. F. G. Masterman He was an innovating Home Secretary to begin
with, and he was a very compassionate person, you know. I mean –
oh, a thing I didn't hear of actually, because it was a matter of
detail, till later – there were a lot of old convicts who'd been back
again and again and again – they were never going to go straight,
and they'd never get a job. Well, he arranged that at Parkhurst
there was a special sitting-room for them with armchairs.

Another different thing was – I don't say he ever contemplated
getting rid of the capital punishment, but he couldn't sleep the
night before an execution.

Robert Blake In 1911 Churchill became First Lord of the Admiralty. He
was on any view a brilliant and far-sighted Minister. He was
responsible for many important Naval reforms. But he continued to
be obsessive about his own office, a point Lucy Masterman underlines.

Mrs C. F. G. Masterman When he got to the Admiralty, he became
really rather a terror to his colleagues because he was always
talking about the Navy and that sort of thing. And Lloyd George
complained that he got him in a corner and kept on talking about
'his blasted ships', which Lloyd George was not particularly
interested in.

Robert Blake Thus we have a picture of him before 1914 as a vigorous,
energetic, no doubt troublesome and argumentative young middle-
aged man clearly on his way up. He had made all the right moves –

perhaps unconsciously rather than by deliberate design – but highly successfully. On the face of things, war, for which so much of his career had prepared him, ought to have consolidated his position. In fact it did just the opposite.

His grand design for victory was the Dardanelles expedition – an attempt to break through to Constantinople, knock out the Turks and secure a supply route to Russia. But he had no real support from the Cabinet. Lord Boothby who later, as a young Conservative M.P., was one of Churchill's few devoted friends in the inter-war years, comments on Churchill's role over the Dardanelles.

Lord Boothby I think the Dardanelles, which has been hailed in the past as the great strategic conception of the First World War and there's truth in that, was very badly bungled and I think that the fault primarily was Churchill's, because he tried to undertake a hazardous major operation of war from what he himself has described as a subordinate position, and to run the whole thing. In fact he did say in summing the whole thing up, 'Men are ill-advised to attempt such ventures from my position'.

Robert Blake There can be endless controversy about the merits of the Dardanelles campaign. There can be little doubt that its failure greatly damaged Churchill's reputation. When Asquith felt obliged to form a coalition government with the Conservatives in May 1915, Churchill's removal from the Admiralty was made an absolute condition by Bonar Law the Conservative leader. Churchill was shunted into a minor office, resigned at the end of the year and rejoined the army.

He soon returned to politics, but when the great political crisis of December 1916 occurred, and Asquith was ousted and Lloyd George, Churchill's friend, became Prime Minister, Churchill – much to his mortification – was not included in the new government. Six months later, he was made Minister of Munitions, but this had ceased by then to be a key office.

However, after the end of the war, in Lloyd George's new coalition from 1918 to 1922 Churchill was first Minister for War and Air, and then for the Colonies. His stock seemed to be rising. Yet in spite of this he did many things which inspired doubts. And he began to acquire a reputation – very unfair no doubt, but none the less damaging – for being a warmonger. Sir Oswald Mosley, who after service in the war entered Parliament in 1918, describes his own doubts about Churchill.

Sir Oswald Mosley I believe him to be personally an entirely honest, genuine and magnanimous character but he had a certain emotional and impulsive instability. My mistrust of him arose from his inveterate drive towards war.

Coming out of the First War after experience in the fighting of the air and trenches, and the loss of all my companions, my obsession, if you like, was to avoid another war. And Churchill, immediately after that war in Mesopotamia, now called Iraq, in his Russian adventure, his attempt – ineffective attempt – to crush Bolshevism in its early days, in Chenak, which was as much or more the fault of Lloyd George, seemed to me continually driving towards war.

Robert Blake Churchill, however, possessed a charm which even his critics found hard to resist.

Sir Oswald Mosley remembers one of his own parliamentary exchanges with Churchill.

Sir Oswald Mosley I remember on one occasion when a debate fell very flat, and I was speaking for the Labour Party, and got up at the end of the debate and made a rather flashy noisy speech, and Churchill had to wind up for the Government. He began rather laboriously in his fashion, 'How disastrous was the day for the Labour Party, all was lost,' and the rest of it, and then he said ' . . . and at the end, on this stricken field forth springs our young Astyanax, the hope of Troy', you see, and everybody roared with laughter. And the joke was entirely turned on me.

And I was very puzzled because I thought, he's never read a line of Homer in his life – how on earth did he pull this one on me ? So I was walking through the Lobby afterwards, and up he came rolling along and grinning in his way, dug me in the ribs and said 'My boy *Bartlett's Popular Quotations* – never be without them!'

And, you know, that was part of his charm, which endeared him to the younger generation. There was absolutely no humbug about him. He hated what he called the goody-goodies and all the rest of it.

Robert Blake This charm did not prevent Churchill acquiring an aura of mistrust which remained with him for many years. It was not diminished by his second change of party. In 1922 he lost office with the fall of the Lloyd-George Coalition and he lost his seat at the ensuing general election.

He decided, rightly, that the Liberals had no future. After various vicissitudes including standing for Parliament under the tongue-twisting title of an Anti-Socialist Constitutionalist, he was offered the post of Chancellor by Baldwin in 1924. He accepted with alacrity and, so the story goes, under the impression that he was being made Chancellor of the Duchy of Lancaster, not, as Baldwin meant, Chancellor of the Exchequer.

Lord Boothby, who was Churchill's Parliamentary private secretary at the time, is critical of Churchill's period in office.

Lord Boothby Oh, very bad Chancellor of the Exchequer. His whole objective was to reduce the income tax by a shilling, which was quite unnecessary because everybody was very well off – or rather the rich were very well off then and there was no need for it.

And he didn't really understand monetary policy or finance policy. He once said to me, 'If only these Treasury fellows and the city bankers who come and see me were admirals or generals, I could talk to them in their own language, and make them do what I wanted. But after a time, they start talking Persian and then I'm sunk!'

Robert Blake A similar view is held by Sir Oswald Mosley, who feels that Churchill was very much under the sway of the Treasury officials.

Sir Oswald Mosley Churchill came to the problem of that kind, the return to the Gold Standard and the rest of it, knowing little, the prisoner of the party, and unable to go against the orthodox opinion.

I think it's fair to say that he knew little in light of his famous observation that unemployment had no more to do with the Gold Standard than the Gulf Stream, which is only equalled by his father's exclamation at the Treasury as Chancellor of the Exchequer when confronted for the first time with the mysteries of the decimal system, in asking 'What are those damned dots?' The strong point of the Churchill family was never economics.

Robert Blake It does not follow that such criticisms of Churchill as Chancellor are fully justified. A case can be made in his defence, and he was certainly responsible for many improvements in social services. But the point is that these adverse opinions were very widely held. Lord Boothby makes a further point about Churchill's determination to reduce income tax.

Lord Boothby This passion to get the income tax down led to the ludicrous ten year rule that he laid down as Chancellor that there would be no war and no war was to be contemplated for ten years and this was to be advanced progressively from year to year. Then he scaled down our naval and military forces and airforce to practically nil.

It's forgotten now, but the truth is that that was the basis of our weakness in the 1930s. Churchill disarmed the country between 1925 and 1930 as nobody's ever disarmed this country before.

Robert Blake Another point that counted against Churchill at this time was his behaviour during the General Strike of 1926. Here is Lord Citrine, who was General Secretary of the T.U.C. at that time.

Lord Citrine We scarcely ever saw Churchill face to face during the strike, and we could only judge his conduct by what we saw in the *British Gazette*, the paper which he controlled on behalf of the Government. And it was vicious to an extreme.

I was told later, only a few years ago, by Lord Davidson, who really edited that paper, that some of the things that Churchill wanted him to put in the paper, and insisted upon him putting in the paper, made his blood boil. And he refused to do it. On occasions he got in touch with the Government to take Baldwin and the Government's decision as to whether such things should be said.

Robert Blake Some years later Lord Citrine sat next to Churchill at dinner, and talked to him about the General Strike.

Lord Citrine I said to him, 'You didn't believe all that rubbish you put in the *British Gazette* about our trying to break the constitution'.

'Oh yes', he said, 'I did. I was in the country when the strike started and I saw red. I thought this must be revolution. And I came back to London,' he said, 'determined to fight it.'

Robert Blake The Conservatives were defeated in the election of 1929. Churchill in opposition parted company with Baldwin on the question whether to support the Labour Party and the Conservative Viceroy of India, Lord Halifax, in their policy of dominion status and self-government for India. Churchill resigned from the Shadow Cabinet on the Indian question, and when the overwhelmingly Conservative Coalition of 1931 was formed under Ramsay MacDonald, he was not invited to join.

No doubt the leaders were glad to have the excuse; but it would be difficult to deny that Churchill had brought it on himself, at least to a very considerable extent. And he made his position worse by persisting in his intemperate opposition to the India Bill long after it was futile to do so, and then by his attitude in supporting King Edward VIII, the Duke of Windsor, during the abdication crisis.

Lord Boothby He didn't understand the reaction of the ordinary man in the street. He had no real sympathy with his aspirations, with his prejudices, with his hopes and with his fears. Churchill was an extraordinary man and he had no knowledge of the ordinary man at all. That, you see, accounts for his frightful misjudgement over the abdication. I mean, he just misjudged the whole temper and feeling of the people over the abdication, and it was another example of a blunder, of a colossal error of judgement; and that finished him. The abdication crisis finished him in this country politically.

And that's why, after that, when he became increasingly aware of the growing menace of Hitler, and demanded re-armament on the greatest scale in this country and especially in the air, and all his warnings were completely justified by events, they were disregarded because he himself was disregarded. But he brought it on himself by the tremendous errors of judgement that he'd made on big issues where he'd completely misjudged the feelings of the man in the street.

Robert Blake The result was that Churchill was not listened to even when he was in the right. Lord Boothby sums up parliamentary opinion about him.

Lord Boothby I would say that from 1937 to 1939, his influence in the House of Commons was about zero, and his friends amounted to about four, of whom I was one.

You see, people remembered a lot of things, and he was associated with a whole series of failures which people put down to lack of judgement. And therefore I would say they didn't distrust him personally, but they distrusted his judgement.

Robert Blake The truth was that Churchill seemed, both to the man in

the street and to the average M.P. of all parties, an erratic dangerous
figure, too ambitious, too pushing, too much on the personal make.
This impression may well have been unfair, but it was at least in
part Churchill's own fault that it existed.

In addition he was associated in people's minds with certain
major blunders or errors of judgement. In a parliamentary democracy it is essential to inspire trust and confidence. Churchill did
not – anyway in peace time when nothing very much seemed to be
happening.

It is perhaps in this contrast between the war-time and the
peace-time Prime Minister that the key to Churchill's career can be
found. It is true that even in the First World War he had been
associated with a major failure, the Dardanelles. But as time went
on, it somehow became muffled, mainly by Churchill's own
eloquent defence of his conduct.

And when war broke out in 1939 he was shown to have been
right on one supreme issue if on no others – the danger of Hitler
and German rearmament. It is not surprising that most people
reversed their opinion of him almost overnight.

Sir Oswald Mosley The English people supported him and they were
right in this sense. If they wanted a war and had a war, or thought
it necessary, he was obviously the man for it – the only man who
over years had trained himself for that purpose, the only man with
the character, with the dynamism to see it through among the people
who thought that a war was necessary.

And therefore he was a man of emergency, and not a man of
normal times, and the British people in broad judgement were
right not to employ him in the first position normally, but to
employ him only abnormally, which a war was.

Robert Blake Churchill himself agreed that had it not been for the
Second World War – ironically, the one enormous stroke of luck
or chance in his career that operated in his favour – he would never
have reached the top.

Lord Boothby Luck played a terrific part. He said to me in 1940, 'It
took Armageddon to make me Prime Minister'; and it did. And
whether you can call the Second World War luck, I should doubt,
but at any rate for Churchill there's no question that the outbreak
of the Second World War brought him to supreme power and that

if that war hadn't happened, he never would have attained supreme
power.

Robert Blake We have seen what went wrong with him in peace time.
But we should not forget that he did get to the top and that he was
one of the greatest statesmen in our history. What was his great
virtue? What was the justification of the confidence ultimately
reposed in him?

Lord Boothby Oh undoubtedly, without any question at all, courage. He
had absolute moral and absolute physical courage and that flamed
up, flared up for all the world to see in 1940. Because there he
really was up against it, and the world thought we were beaten, and
his courage was imparted to the British people in the most extraordinary way, and I think it saved us.

And I never knew any occasion in his life when he wasn't
absolutely dauntless, especially in the face of adversity. I think
that his supreme quality was courage. Imagination up to a point,
but imagination very often led him wrong to wrong judgements
and wrong conclusions, but the courage was always there. I should
say it certainly was his supreme quality.

8 The Way to the Top

Dr Norman Hunt In this final programme of the series *Personality and Power* we're going to look at some of the factors, both political and psychological, which help to produce successful political leaders. We've already tried in these programmes to examine the careers of seven specific twentieth-century leaders and how they got to the top; Baldwin, Franklin Roosevelt, Winston Churchill, Khrushchev, Mussolini, Nehru and Nkrumah. In particular we were concerned with certain special questions about them – what personal qualities and drives helped them along, how ambitious they were, how carefully they planned their political careers, how far luck played a part in their success and how far, if at all, they changed the rules of the political game to help their own advancement.

Well, we are now going to look at all these issues and some extra psychiatric ones too, not only in terms of the seven people we've already covered in these programmes but also of political success in general. In fact we're going to try to identify what common elements, if any, go into the making of political leaders.

With me now in the studio to discuss this, there's first of all Professor Asa Briggs, the historian and social scientist, who's Vice-Chancellor of Sussex University. And our second guest is Dr Anthony Storr, the writer and psychiatrist.

Gentlemen, it seems to me that we ought to make it clear first of all about the seven men we're focusing on in this discussion that they succeeded in fact in four completely different political and constitutional situations. I mean for example Baldwin, Roosevelt and Churchill; they achieved their power in stable democratic systems and they achieved it by normal constitutional means. Now Mussolini, in contrast, took over power when a democratic system was crumbling; and then Nkrumah and Nehru took over power from an imperial government, an imperial régime that was giving up power. And then, fourthly, Khrushchev took over power in a continuing system but it was a continuing communist one. Do you think it's important to make that categorisation. Asa Briggs ?

Professor Asa Briggs I think it's very useful to look at these situations side by side. But I think there are two other points I'd want to make. The first is as a historian and the second, if you like, as a social scientist.

First, I think that all the people we're talking about belonged to the same period of time, even though they were in different situations. All of them were forced in some sense or other to take account of what we would call, in jargon terms, 'the people'. None of them could take authority for granted in the same sense that a dynasty with family power passed on from one generation to another could take it for granted and I think that this commonness of the situation is important.

Secondly, in terms of social science I think it is very valuable indeed to try to bring personality back into politics, not merely to look at tendencies, trends, quantitative assessments, but also to try to look at the way in which people do react in the situations in which they find themselves. And I think that all these seven do raise very intersting inter-disciplinary questions in this connection.

Dr Anthony Storr Well of course I'm very glad you said that about bringing personality back into politics because one of the things that strikes me is the interest there is and the lack of knowledge we have about the relation between the type of personality that's thrown up under special social circumstances. If you've got a particular kind of hopelessness, then you tend to get a particular type of leader. If you've got a particular type of crisis, then you get a particular type of person thrown up, like for instance Churchill. And it's the interaction between the social state of the community as it were and the type of leader that you get thrown up which I think is a very interesting thing which very little is known about.

Dr Norman Hunt Well before we go on to discuss this, I'd like to introduce a new hypothesis about the psychological make-up of the political power seekers. It's been put to us by Dr Gerald Woolfson who's a consultant psychiatrist himself.

He points out that it's too tentative to describe it as a theory, particularly when our knowledge of the real personalities of public figures is very limited – in fact some of our knowledge is based on anecdotes which may well be of doubtful authenticity. Much of it rests on retrospective rationalisation by biographers and by the leaders themselves, and these sources may not truly represent the reality of their inner private lives. In fact our opinions on their private lives are bound to be to some extent impressionistic based on an average of collective judgement.

But despite this, says Dr Woolfson, some widely acceptable conclusions can be drawn.

Dr Gerald Woolfson There seems to be general agreement among psychologists about the character traits required by politicians to reach the top.

The most important of these traits is clearly a very high intelligence; without this, I think, it's almost impossible to succeed in politics.

Successful politicians seem to have the ability to cope with a high degree of stress and uncertainty, and to resist the antagonistic feelings of others.

They are able to project self-confidence and they have a charismatic personality with a high verbal fluency. Many of them are able to use this gift of rhetoric, coupled with emotionalism, to sway large numbers of people in a demagogic way.

Others have a tremendous strength in resisting pressures to conform. They may be dominating and aggressive, or ruthless if the occasion calls for it.

They have the ability to differentiate finely between effective and ineffective colleagues and again be able to ruthlessly eliminate them if it is necessary.

And finally the successful politician must have an unwavering belief and an intense commitment to his own views or the collective ideologies of his party, and be able to implement whatever he wants to do with great determination.

Dr Norman Hunt These character traits, as Gerald Woolfson points out, are not particularly subtle or controversial. And of course each individual's idiosyncratic psychological development is of the utmost importance in determining his adult style of life, personal drives, compensations for unresolved conflicts and aggressions, and so on. But Woolfson also believes that almost all those who achieve great political power fall into one or a combination of three major personality types.

Dr Gerald Woolfson I believe that most politicians who achieve great power – and this includes the seven who have been discussed in these programmes – are composite personalities who fit into one or more of the following personality categories.

Firstly, the obsessional: he is the man who is the hard task-master. He is conscientious and diligent, persistent in perfecting the knowledge expected of him or idiosyncratically chosen by him. He is the steady plodder, rigid, inflexible, often doctrinaire and a lover of order and discipline. This kind of man rarely achieves the highest order of power because of his lack of imagination and unwillingness to take risks. Not unnaturally, very few successful politicians fit into this category. However, there are some, for example Baldwin, who contained many of the elements of this personality type.

Secondly, there is the personality type which I style the control-led hypermanic. This kind of personality is lively, confident, soci-able and his relative euphoria may be obvious and infectious to all. He's often irritable, an extrovert, ebullient and talkative with a powerful charisma, commanding affection and making rapport easily. He seems to burn with an inner fire and is like a dynamo, possessed of unlimited physical and mental energy. For example, Khrushchev and Mussolini and even Churchill and Roosevelt possessed many of these characteristics.

And then finally, and most interesting of all, is the controlled sociopathic personality. This kind of person may be or appear to be socially well-adjusted. But behind his façade of social con-formity, bonhomie and even tolerance, he is basically a ruthless, calculating, devious and cunning man. He is Machiavellian in his cynical, intrinsically detached and destructive attitudes. He is manipulative, calm and often pitiless, and he may too be paranoid and irritable. He is the kind of person who is willing to sacrifice friends and colleagues on the altar of his ambition. But the impor-tant thing is that he does it in such a clever way that few, if any, know or notice how he is manipulating people or situations.

Dr Norman Hunt Well gentlemen, there perhaps is a starting point for us. How far are political leaders a mixture of these three personality types? The obsessional, plodding along steadily, the controlled hypermanic, as Woolfson said, like a dynamo possessing almost unlimited physical and mental energy, and perhaps the most important and sinister from our point of view, the sociopath, basically ruthless, calculating and devious and so clever in manipulating people and situations that few realise that he's doing it, indeed in some cases he doesn't fully realise it himself.

Dr Anthony Storr Well, as Dr Woolfson points out in his classification, I think it's rather rare for obsessional personalities to get to the top because on the whole they're not very decisive. They always see both sides of questions and therefore they don't act in the way that is necessary if you are going to achieve great power.

I agree entirely that the controlled hypermanic is a very common kind of personality. What Dr Woolfson hadn't time to mention is of course that the people who behave in this way like dynamos – and Churchill was certainly one – was that they daren't stop because if they stop, they tend to get very depressed – the opposite side of the manic personality.

And as regards the sociopath, I think these are essentially the paranoid people, the people who have to have a sort of 'anti-Christ', an enemy that they are out to defeat, and it seems to me that those are the people who get thrown up in times of great misery like after the Black Death or in Germany for instance during the period between the wars when inflation was rampant. And then it is that you get these paranoid psychopathic people coming to the top, like Hitler.

Dr Norman Hunt Asa Briggs, how many of these particular leaders in your view were sociopaths?

Professor Asa Briggs Oh, I think very few of them were sociopaths in the terms in which this has been defined. I'm a bit uneasy about the three personality types, although I can see the value of starting from these, almost if you like as ideal types or special types.

First of all, I entirely agree with Anthony Storr that obsessional types wouldn't normally get to the top. I don't think that Baldwin incidentally was an obsessional type in any sense of the word at all. I think there was a certain laziness about Baldwin, a certain un-willingness to reach decisions which was pointed out in the programme about him. I think you've really got to explain Baldwin essentially in terms of the social situation, rather than in terms of any abnormal psychology at all.

As far as the second type, the hypermanics are concerned, obviously they do play an immense part in the history of mankind. I doubt whether they need all be quite as extrovert as implied. I think there's a good deal of introversion, certainly in the spells of withdrawal if you like from frenetic activity on the part of these. I would have thought there were very important introvert elements, let us say, in Nkrumah.

Dr Anthony Storr Isn't this just possibly the period of depression?

Professor Asa Briggs It may be the period of depression but I think that some of them in fact were not, in the ordinary sense of the word, associated with what one would call extrovert activities.

And as far as the sociopath element is concerned, I think it's possible in ways to exaggerate the destructiveness of this. I'm sure that the destructiveness is fundamental – there is an inherent nihilism in it – and yet, at the same time, the quest for monument-alism – to produce something which is on a very big, almost super-human scale – can produce through this type in politics, I think, elements of the attempt to provide something eternal in a very rapidly changing society. You've got to have big public works, you've got to have enormous displays – colonnades and so on – and I think that this type in politics isn't always associated entirely with destruction. There are dreams, if you like, of creative grandeur of the sort that we associate with Hitler.

Dr Norman Hunt I just wonder myself about this question of ability and intelligence, because one of the things that strikes me about the leaders that we have particularly under the microscope – the Baldwins, the Roosevelts, the Churchills, Nkrumahs and so on – is that some of them, at any rate, I wouldn't have put in the category of outstanding intellectual ability – that is I wouldn't have put Baldwin in that category, I'm not sure I would have put Roosevelt in that category, nor would I have put Churchill in that category; all people with in a sense very moderate academic attainments, in so far as academic attainments are some measure of intellectual capacity.

Professor Asa Briggs Well, I think one must avoid all feeling that academic attainments really carry with them some kind of special priority. I don't think any of these men, any of them, really was intelligent in the sense that we would want to talk about intelligence, in terms of the creative intelligence of modern scholarship and learning.

I think that they were all very shrewd and they had got an understanding of the relationship between means and ends, even if they defied it sometimes because of their own psychological dispositions. I agree that I wouldn't call them intelligent.

Nor do I think that they were all people who were able to resist the antagonistic feelings of others. Some of them, I think, were extremely sensitive men who were terribly afraid of what other people said about them, but they could really convert this feeling, if you like, of dissatisfaction and antagonism on the part of others into a very powerful motor of their own political activity.

Dr Anthony Storr I entirely agree about the high I.Q. I don't think this is a necessity. But I think one of Dr Woolfson's other characteristics, the high verbal fluency, is a very striking characteristic, and of course one that doesn't correlate with general intelligence necessarily. It's extraordinary how people can be terribly fluent and not very bright.

But as regards resisting antagonism, I couldn't help thinking that one of the characteristics of these people was really what psychoanalysts talk of as infantile omnipotence. They are so sure they're right and that's what's so extraordinary. I mean, here you have a number of people perhaps who haven't been terribly distinguished in youth and perhaps like Churchill have been terribly backward at school and so on. And yet, they're absolutely sure that they know better than other people. And that, I think, accounts for their ability to resist antagonists, even if they appear to conform to what other people want and their commitment to their own views and their ruthlessness, and their charisma, because nothing gets across to other people like somebody who knows he's right.

Dr Norman Hunt Yes, that is one of the interesting things about this – all of them, as you say, were convinced they were right. And yet they were all from very different social origins, that is if you think in terms of Baldwin, Churchill, very much out of the top drawer, Roosevelt, very much out of the top drawer with all the possible advantages. On the other hand, Krushchev, Mussolini and Nkrumah not so. Is there any significance in that do you think, Asa Briggs ?

Professor Asa Briggs Yes I think there is. I think that we've got to have a theory not only of motivation or initial impulsion into politics but also of the avenues of political advancement. And it seems to me that the family as an institution provides a link, if you like, between the psychology of the subject and the sociology of the subject, because a family is an institution which through the nexus of relationships and so on, can obviously affect very directly the way in which you get into politics at the start. And some of them used their families very effectively as talismans, or indeed as very real ways in.

But I think that also we've got to distinguish then between people who get into politics through a conception, if you like, of service, which may be rooted in a rather traditionalist view of authority and people who get in deliberately through the feeling of being associated with movement, and indeed with revolution.

And there's an intermediate stage between these two conditions of entry in the idea of the political party, which can at the same time both be a revolutionary party in certain circumstances or a party which is pledged to maintaining some kind of continuous order.

So that I would want in relation to any great man to find out what was the avenue that he chose to move along, and what was the possibility of moving along different avenues. Because I think we've got to ask about many people why it is a political avenue at all that they choose, and if they are going into politics, why it is that they'll hitch themselves to the conception of a revolutionary party rather than hitching themselves to some bits of the establishment, the system as it already is.

Dr Norman Hunt But there does seem to be a distinction doesn't there, Asa Briggs, in this in that those who come from good families with a tradition of service from middle-class or upper middle-class families, seemed to be the ones who flourished in traditional democratic systems, the Roosevelts, the Churchills, the Baldwins – a tradition of service and they do it in traditional democratic systems. Those who've come with a burning desire to change things – the Khrushchevs, the Mussolinis – they come from a very different walk of life, right from the bottom.

Professor Asa Briggs Not true of Nehru, who really is quite different in this respect and I think not true of quite a number of other leaders, and I would doubt if it would be true of the next stage of political leadership which we know nothing about at the moment. All these are creatures of the past already.

Dr Anthony Storr Don't you think we ought to make another distinction which perhaps goes across this? I mean psychiatrists are always accused, sometimes rightly, of attributing motives to people which aren't there and one of the things that psychiatrists sometimes say is that anybody who attains very high office for instance is sort of pathological, that he must have a pathological ambition or something of this kind.

Now I think one's got to distinguish between people who are unusually gifted and able and powerful in themselves – as it were, they have a genetic quality – and people who are over-compensating for an inner sense of inferiority and I think it is possible to distinguish these types. I think one has also got to remember that in our society – in our very large societies – it's quite often true that there are a lot of very able people who don't in fact get enough scope for their abilities and who are looking, like Lord Reith said in that immortal phrase, 'always to be fully stretched', and never finding it. And I think those are a different kind of people from the people who are really over-compensating in my psychiatric, pathological sense.

Dr Norman Hunt Asa Briggs, you were talking a moment or two ago about the importance of power base, or the importance of a tradition of service in the families from which people came. I wonder also how important it is actually to have made the right connections in the early part of your career. Because one of the things that strikes me particularly about the characters that we've got under the microscope is that nearly all of them at the crucial moment had the right connections.

Baldwin owed his rise, for example, to his close friendship with Davidson, which made him Bonar Law's Parliamentary Private Secretary and then being next to Bonar Law, this enabled him to get the leg-up. Khrushchev started out because he was a protegé of Kaganovich, and this was absolutely crucial in his career. As far as Nehru was concerned, if it hadn't been for the close connection with Gandhi, Nehru wouldn't have been the great figure that we have.

All these people – or virtually all of them – had the right connection at an early point in their career, and without it they wouldn't have succeeded.

Professor Asa Briggs Oh, I think this is certainly true. I call these people the helpers, if you like. There are certain people who attract helpers more easily than others. I think there are aspects of the psychology of the people that we've been looking at in this series which do explain the fact that they found helpers at particular stages of their careers. There are some people who'd never find helpers at all, in any society at any period of time. I think that these were all very effective in being able to find people who would back them. But those people were looking for certain qualities which were already there.

One aspect of all these people, I think, is that they could engage at certain stages in their life in a kind of double talk or double think. It was perfectly possible for them, if you like, to dissimulate the full range of their ambitions and ideas at certain stages and to bring them out fully later on, after they'd got into power or on the way to power. They were never really, as far as the helpers were concerned, revealing the whole range of their potential but they were making the helpers feel that these were people who were worth backing.

Dr Anthony Storr There's another point in that, isn't there, in the question of timing? I mean it's not only a question of having the right connections with people but it's a question of what one of our chief students of the corridors of power, C. P. Snow, calls 'the ability to be present at the right time' and he makes one of his characters in one of his books say, 'Never be too proud to be there!' You've got to be on the spot, and even if you're out of office for years, like Churchill or other people, you've got to be around and you've got to make sure that people notice you. And this is a question of timing rather than of having the right connections with people.

Dr Norman Hunt Isn't this also in part not just a question of timing but

7

your own personality and your own aims and objectives at the right moment falling within the mood of the period, within the mood of the times?

In other words, Baldwin managed to have great success because passivity was a great reaction against Lloyd George's dynamism, which people were rather tired of. Roosevelt in America came in just at the time when people wanted action to clear up the mess of the depression and so on.

Professor Asa Briggs Yes I agree with this; but it's terribly difficult to define a phrase like 'the mood of the time'. I think that there are contrasting styles of leadership in successive generations. This is part of the psychological problem of the relationship between one generation and another. After you've had a man like Lloyd George, then you are likely in certain respects to get a man like Baldwin.

I think also that part of this explanation of mood of the time needs to be related to the methods of communication. All these people were able, in relation to the circumstances in which they found themselves, to deal with the new aspects of communication pretty effectively, to get away from accepted notions of oratory into rather new forms of oratory in certain cases. And I feel that none of them really would be men of the television age, none of them would be men of the age of computers, that they are already historical figures, if you like, in relation to the twentieth century, which is still changing.

Dr Norman Hunt You were talking earlier, Anthony Storr, on this point. You talked about their high verbal fluency, and of course it's true that Roosevelt and Baldwin were particularly effective through radio. But I wonder if you agree with Asa Briggs' point that none of these figures would have had the ability to communicate in a more modern television age. It seems to me that's rather doubtful.

Dr Anthony Storr I don't know. I should have thought you can be trained to that to some extent. I still think high verbal fluency's important even on television. It does matter to some extent what you look like, unfortunately, but I think the high verbal fluency still holds and provided you've got that, I should have thought the rest of the technique of television broadcasting was fairly easily learned.

Professor Asa Briggs Oh, I could imagine Nkrumah on television without the least difficulty and indeed some of the other characters. I'm not arguing that they wouldn't have been interested in television. All I'm merely saying is that each one of these figures, in his own time, appreciated the communications context in which he found himself and he appreciated it instinctively in some kind of way, and not simply through calculation.

Dr Norman Hunt I wonder if one can draw a distinction at all here between the sort of people who managed to get to the top and achieve power in democratic systems of government, and the sort of people who do it in totalitarian or authoritarian systems. Because one of the things that struck me from these programmes was the emphasis in the democratic systems, particularly about Baldwin and Franklin Roosevelt, that the way they got to the top was because in their earlier careers they specifically gave no offence to anybody. They were all things to all men. They were not great dynamic men of particular ideas.

Now one doesn't feel in the authoritarian systems, that the Nkrumahs and Krushchevs got to the top because they'd actually got something to do or say. . . .

Professor Asa Briggs But nor did Lloyd George in England or Wales, or wherever it was. I mean, my own feeling. . . .

Dr Norman Hunt Yes, but could I just come in on that. I think Lloyd George is a very good example. He gets to the top at a moment of crisis. Churchill is the same. The man who can get to the top in a democracy with ideas and vigour, and who has made enemies beforehand, gets to the top in a moment of crisis.

Professor Asa Briggs This may well be true. And it may well have been that there was a moment of crisis in a kind of a concealed way when Khrushchev came into power. But I think that Lloyd George and Khrushchev had certain peasant qualities in common. I feel that the difference between the systems may to some extent be exaggerated, although I think it's a very important element to examine in each individual case.

Dr Anthony Storr I'm sure you couldn't survive in Soviet Russia without being a lot more ruthless than we would stand in England for any of our leaders.

Dr Norman Hunt We've talked a bit every now and then about the importance of creed or philosophy. But I just wonder how important it really is because again somebody like Baldwin or a Franklin Roosevelt managed to achieve power without really having a creed or a philosophy.

Roosevelt, although we associate the New Deal with him, didn't know about it when he actually took power, it was something that was pragmatically worked out afterwards. And as far as Nkrumah was concerned, it was nationalism. In other words, the creed doesn't seem to be particularly important in producing men in power.

Professor Asa Briggs Not I think in the sense of a philosophical creed or an ideology. But I think it's essential that they must be able to see certain kinds of connection, rational or irrational, between different aspects of life; and I think that they all in different ways succeeded in this, perhaps Roosevelt less than most. I think that Roosevelt probably didn't have any very strong views even though he was drawn through the situation in which he found himself into appearances of strength, which were sometimes more appearances than realities.

Dr Anthony Storr I think ideologists tend to get power as I said earlier, really in times of misery and frustration and hopelessness. And then I think an ideology is important, because it's very important to have a scape-goat, an enemy that you can blame, like the Jews or somebody or other, for the state of society. And people fall for this if they're miserable enough and under those conditions, a passionate ideologist gets power which he would never get, thank God, in the ordinary state of affairs in a western democracy.

Dr Norman Hunt One of the things in the end though that strikes me about all this, that at these particular times with the Churchills, the Roosevelts and so on, there were plenty of people around in these societies, who'd got the same abilities, the same ability to communicate, the same sense of drive and so on.

And yet in the end, the crucial thing was the question of luck, that the Roosevelts and the Baldwins and the Nehrus and all the rest of them were in the right place at the right time, and that luck was perhaps the most important factor in all in explaining why they got to the top.

Professor Asa Briggs That's why we still need historians as well as social scientists, I think, to describe the particularities of history. I think all these men in their different ways believed in luck. Churchill believed in the stars, he believed in his destiny. So, I believe, did Nkrumah. Mussolini had a certain kind of self-awareness which I think distinguished him in certain ways from some of the rest. But I think that they all did believe in luck. They were aware of the fact that they were creatures of destiny as well as creatures of history.

Dr Anthony Storr Yes, I think it's important to point out that you can believe you're a creature of destiny and be quite wrong. I mean there are quite a number of people who've been waiting in the wings hoping that Britain will collapse and that they will then be called in to save the situation, who in fact haven't been called in and won't be called in but still continue to believe that they are men of destiny.

Dr Norman Hunt But these people not only believed they were men of destiny, they had the luck too.

Dr Anthony Storr They were there.

Dr Norman Hunt Thank you, gentlemen.

Bibliography

STANLEY BALDWIN

General text books or outline books of the period

MARWICK, A. *Britain in the century of total war* 1968. Bodley Head, £3·15

MOWAT, C. L. *Britain between the wars, 1918-1940* 1968. Methuen, £2·50; paperback £1·50

TAYLOR, A. J. P. *English history, 1914-1945* (Oxford History of England, vol. 15) 1965. O.U.P., £2·50

THOMSON, D. *England in the 20th century* 1964. Cape, £1·75; 1970. Penguin Books, 30p

Books more specifically on Baldwin

BALDWIN, A. W. *My father: the true story* 1955. Allen & Unwin, o.p.

MIDDLEMASS, K. and BARNES, J. *Baldwin* 1969. Weidenfeld and Nicolson, £5·25

RAYMOND, J. ed. *The Baldwin age* 1960. Eyre, o.p.

WILLIAMS, F. *A pattern of rulers* 1965. Longmans, £2·25

YOUNG, G. M. *Stanley Baldwin* 1952. Hart-Davis, o.p.

F. D. ROOSEVELT

BURNS, J. M. *Roosevelt: the lion and the fox* 1956. Secker & Warburg, o.p.

EINAUDI, M. *The Roosevelt revolution* 1959. Harcourt, Brace & World Inc., N.Y. $6.50

FLYNN, J. T. *The Roosevelt myth* 1956. Devin-Adair Co., N.Y. $3.95

FREIDEL, F. *Franklin D. Roosevelt* Little, Brown & Co., Mass.
Vol. 1 Apprenticeship 1952. $8.50
Vol. 2 Ordeal 1954. $8.50
Vol. 3 Triumph 1956. $8.50

HOFSTADTER, R. *The American political tradition* 1962. Cape, £1·75; 1967. paperback £1·10. For essay on F. D. Roosevelt

LEUCHTENBURG, W. E. *Franklin D. Roosevelt and the New Deal, 1932-40* (Torchbooks) 1963. Harper & Row, £3·70; paperback £1·15

PERKINS, F. *The Roosevelt I knew* (Colophon) 1965. Harper & Row, £1·30

SCHLESINGER, A. M. *The age of Roosevelt* Heinemann.
Vol. 1 *The crisis of the old order, 1911-33* 1957. o.p.
Vol. 2 *The coming of the New Deal* 1960. o.p.
Vol. 3 *The policies of upheaval* 1961. o.p.

TUGWELL, R. G. *The democratic Roosevelt* 1969. Penguin Books, o.p.

NIKITA KHRUSHCHEV

CONQUEST, R. *Russia after Khrushchev* 1965. Pall Mall P, £2·50

CRANKSHAW, E. *Khrushchev* 1966. Collins, o.p.

FAINSOD, M. *How Russia is ruled* 2nd edition 1963. Harvard U.P.: O.U.P., £4·50

FRANKLAND, M. *Khrushchev* 1966. Penguin Books, 25p

TATU, M. *Power in the Kremlin* 1968. Collins, £4·20

BENITO MUSSOLINI

FERMI, L. *Mussolini* 1961. Univ. Chicago Press, £3·50; 1966 Phoenix Books, £1·35

FINER, H. *Mussolini's Italy* 1964. F. Cass, £4·50

HIBBERT, C. *Benito Mussolini* 1962. Longmans, £2; 1965. Penguin Books, o.p.

KIRKPATRICK, Sir I. A. *Mussolini* 1964. Odhams P., o.p.

MEGARO, G. *Mussolini in the making* 1967. Fertig, Howard, Inc., N.Y. $11.

MUSSOLINI, B. *My Autobiography* 1936. Pater Noster Library, o.p.

PANDIT NEHRU

BRECHER, M. *Nehru: a political biography* 1959. O.U.P. o.p.; abridged edn. 1961. paperback, 40p

NANDA, B. R. *The Nehrus* 1962. Allen & Unwin, £2·50

NEHRU, J. *An autobiography* 1952. J. Lane, o.p.; 1965. Paragon, paperback $2.50

NEHRU, J. *A bunch of old letters* 1960. Asia Publishing House, £1·60

NEHRU, J. *The discovery of India* 4th edn. 1956. Meridian Books, o.p.; 1965. Asia Publishing House, paperback, £1·40.

TAHMANKAR, D. J. *Sardar Patel* 1970. Allen & Unwin, £3.

KWAME NKRUMAH

AFRIFA, A. A. *The Ghana coup: 24th February* 1966. F. Cass, reprinting due June 1971

AUSTIN, D. *Politics in Ghana 1946-60* 1964. R.I.I.A.: O.U.P. £3·15; paperback £1·40

BRETTON, H. L. *The rise and fall of Kwame Nkrumah* 1967. Pall Mall P., o.p.

FITCH, B. and OPPENHEIMER, M. *Ghana: end of an illusion* 1966. Monthly Review Press, £1·25; paperback 63p

NKRUMAH, K. *Ghana: an autobiography* ed. by E. Powell 1957. Nelson, o.p.

TIMOTHY, B. *Kwame Nkrumah: his rise to power* 2nd edn. 1963. Allen & Unwin, o.p.

SIR WINSTON CHURCHILL

BONHAM-CARTER, Lady V. *Winston Churchill, as I knew him* 1965. Eyre and Spottiswoode and Collins, £2·25

CHURCHILL, R. S. *Winston S. Churchill* Heinemann.
  Vol. 1 *Youth, 1874-1900* 1966. £3·15
  Vol. 2 *The young politician, 1901-14* 1967. £3·15
companion Vol. 1 in 2 parts. 1967. £7 set
companion Vol. 2 in 3 parts. 1969. £10·50

CHURCHILL, Sir W. S. *The Second World War* 6 vols. 1948-54. Cassell, £3 each; 12 vols. 1964. paperback 40p each

CHURCHILL, Sir W. S. *The world crisis 1911-18* vol. 1 and 2 (Mentor Books) 1968. New English Library, 52½p each

JAMES, R. RHODES *Churchill: a study in failure, 1900-1939* 1970. Weidenfeld and Nicolson, £3·15

THE WAY TO THE TOP

ADORNO, T. W. and others *The authoritarian personality* 1950. Harper and Row, £4·55

EYSENCK, H. J. *The psychology of politics* 1954. Routledge & Kegan Paul, £2·50

GUTTSMAN, W. L. *British political elite* 1964. MacGibbon & Kee, £2·50

KRETSCHMER, E. *Physique and character* 1936. Routledge & Kegan Paul, o.p.; 2nd edn. 1951. Humanities P., $4

MacIVER, R. M. *Power transformed* 1964. Collier-Macmillan, o.p.

MILLS, C. WRIGHT *Power elite* 1956. N.Y.: O.U.P. £4; paperback 90p

OLIVER, F. S. *The endless adventure: personalities and practical politics in eighteenth century England* 3 vols. 1930-35 A.M.S. Press, Inc. N.Y. $47.50

RUSSELL, B. *Power* 1938. Allen & Unwin, reprinting, no date; paperback 30p

SAMPSON, R. V. *Equality and power* 1965. Heinemann Educational, £1·75; paperback, reprinting, no date.

SHELDON, W. H. *Varieties of temperament* 1942. Harper & Row, o.p.

Notes on the Contributors

KWESI ARMAH Lawyer, diplomat and politician. Ghana's High Commissioner in London 1961-5. Minister of Trade 1965.

ADOLF BERLE (Died 1971) U.S. Assistant Secretary of State 1938-44. Lawyer, diplomat and political colleague of President F. D. Roosevelt.

LORD BOOTHBY Politician and TV personality. Conservative M.P. 1924-58. Friend and colleague of Winston Churchill during much of his career.

LORD BROCKWAY Labour M.P. 1929-31. 1950-64. Writer, politician and anti-colonial propagandist.

PROFESSOR SIR GEORGE CATLIN Writer, historian and political scientist.

LORD CITRINE General Secretary of the Trades Union Congress 1926-46.

EDWARD CRANKSHAW Writer, and expert on Soviet affairs. Biographer of Khrushchev.

VISCOUNTESS DAVIDSON Conservative M.P. 1937-59. Created Life Peeress 1963 as Baroness Northchurch. A lifelong friend of the Baldwin family and widow of J. C. C. Davidson – later Viscount Davidson – a close political associate of Stanley Baldwin for many years.

JAMES FARLEY U.S. Postmaster-General 1933-40. F. D. Roosevelt's campaign manager in 1932 Presidential election. Politician and businessman.

REV. SANDY FRASER Schoolmaster and educational administrator. One of Kwame Nkrumah's teachers at Achimota College. 1927-30.

SIR WILLIAM HAYTER Diplomat and historian. British Ambassador to the U.S.S.R. 1953-57. Warden of New College, Oxford since 1958.

DENIS HEALEY Labour M.P. since 1952. Secretary of State for Defence 1964-70.

MRS LUCY MASTERMAN Widow (and biographer) of C.F.G. Masterman, the Liberal M.P. and Cabinet Minister, who was under secretary to the Home Office when Winston Churchill was Home Secretary.

KRISHNA MENON Statesman and lawyer. India's Minister of Defence, 1957-62.

SAM MORRIS Writer and journalist. Personal press officer to President Nkrumah.

SIR OSWALD MOSLEY Conservative M.P. 1918-22. Independent M.P. 1922-24. Labour M.P. 1924, 1926-31. Chancellor of the Duchy of Lancaster 1929-30. Writer and politician.

FRANKLIN D. ROOSEVELT JUNIOR Youngest son of President F. D. Roosevelt. Lawyer, government official and politician.

IAN STEPHENS Journalist and historian. Editor *The Statesman* (Calcutta and Delhi) 1942-51.

THE EARL OF SWINTON Conservative M.P. 1918-1935. President of the Board of Trade 1922-23, 1924-29, 1931. Secretary of State for the Colonies 1931-35. Secretary of State for Air 1935-38. Minister for Civil Aviation 1944-45. Chancellor of the Duchy of Lancaster and Minister of Materials 1951-52. Secretary of State for Commonwealth Relations 1952-55.

DATTA TAHMANKAR Biographer and journalist. London correspondent *Deccan Herald*.

SIR HARRY VERNEY Liberal M.P. 1910-18. At Harrow with Winston Churchill and later Assistant Private Secretary to Secretary of State for Colonies, Lord Elgin, when Churchill was Under-Secretary of State for the Colonies.

DAVID WILLIAMS Writer and broadcaster on African affairs. Editor *West Africa*.